Medals for the Champions:

Memoirs of a Support Worker

Lola N Guzman

To each of the people I support, especially those who shared their incredible stories with me. You all know who you are. I express my most sincere and enormous gratitude for all that you bring to my life.

To my best friend and soulmate Matthew Warren for his unconditional support and help on this project. Thank you for always being there for me.

To my dear artist friend Juakin Medina for such a beautiful book cover and for inspiring me with your positive energy.

Contents

Foreword

I have been working for more than five years in and around Hertfordshire as a support worker helping adults with learning disabilities. The organisation for which I work and many others share a beautiful philosophy that strives to help create a world where people with learning disabilities are valued equally, listened to and included in society. Part of this work has involved planning and running various activities for the people we support and helping them participate in events ranging from afternoon dances to vacations somewhere special, with the hope that we can bring some joy and laughter to their days.

With the collaboration of some of the people I have had the privilege to support (names have been changed to protect their identities), this book is an opportunity for me to share some of their stories and show how important it is that they are able to receive the care and support we provide. It enables them to achieve their goals in life by promoting independence and helping them make friends, form relationships and engage in their favourite activities and hobbies, giving them a happier life as a result.

While the core message of this book was born from the experiences I have had with the people I support, I also wanted to share the story of how I came to love caring as a profession. A big part of this was growing up with my brother Martin. He lived in a vegetative state until the age of ten due to severe cerebral palsy caused by complications during his birth. I was five when he passed away. My brother's short life had a great impact on my own life while he was alive, and after his death, he has continued to have a powerful influence on me and the path I have walked.

This book also tells of how I ended up working in care homes in England looking after elderly people with dementia and Alzheimer's disease and, for the last five years, in a job that I adore – helping people with learning disabilities. It's a job that brings days full of challenges and difficulties but also many immensely gratifying moments with genuine people who give a purpose to my existence.

My story brought me here, and through the stories of the people I care for, I have learned much. Not just what life is like with disabilities or health problems but also the concerns, desires, frustrations and passions for life that all human beings share regardless of personal circumstances.

"I will lend you, for a little time, a child of mine," He said.
"For you to love the while he lives and mourn for when he's dead.
It may be six or seven years, or twenty-two or three,
But will you, 'till I call him back, take care of him for me?
He'll bring his charms to gladden you, and should his stay be brief,
You'll have his lovely memories as solace for your grief."

"I cannot promise he will stay; since all from earth return,
But there are lessons taught down there I want this child to learn.
I've looked the wide world over in My search for teachers true
And from the throngs that crowd life's lanes I have chosen you.
Now will you give him all your love, not think the labor vain,
Nor hate Me when I come to call to take him back again?"

I fancied that I heard them say, "Dear Lord, Thy will be done!
For all the joy Thy child shall bring, the risk of grief we run.
We'll shelter him with tenderness, we'll love him while we may,
And for the happiness we've known, forever grateful stay;
But should the angels call for him much sooner than we planned,
We'll brave the bitter grief that comes and try to understand!"

Edgar Guest

Martin

I will never forget his vivacious black eyes as they searched the room for me while I sat playing with my toy kitchen set and my dolls. I was three years old, and I didn't understand why he was always lying down. Later, my parents would explain to me that he was ill and would never walk or jump around like other children his age. He was seven. I really didn't care, because he was my brother and I loved him just the way I had always known him. I liked to play next to the bed where he was lying and hear him laugh as I talked to my dolls and pretended to be everyone's mother.

My brother is always there in my mind's eye. I remember him with skin as white as porcelain and as smooth as silk. Brown curly hair covered his small ears, and his lips were rosy and heart shaped. He was long and thin, without any mobility, but he could see and hear perfectly. He was a sharp, piercing observer of everything that caught his attention. He could not speak but would laugh when he was happy, grimace when he was discontented and howl loudly when he was angry or uncomfortable.

My parents were entirely devoted to Martin, especially my mother, who spent most of her time at home while my father worked hard all through the week. He would leave early in the morning and come home for lunch each day before heading back out to work again. He would always return when it was dark; the working day would last for as long as there was usable light. My mother looked after us all throughout the day: Martin, my older brother Lorenzo and me. Lorenzo was twelve years old, and although he was already more independent and did not need as much attention and care as Martin and me, my mother still needed to keep an eye on him. He was reaching his teenage years, and, like many teenagers, he could find trouble in an empty room.

Every morning, my mother's routine would begin with me. She would run the hot water and I would get a good scrub in the bath. She would then prepare breakfast for my brother Lorenzo and corral him into getting ready for school. Once he had left for school, she would turn her attention to Martin's endless care. Every day, she would give him a bed bath because he was too long and awkward for her to move in and out of the bathtub on her own. Sometimes, when my father was around to help, they would move him together. After bath time was over, she would then prepare a soft mash or a bottle for his breakfast.

"Mum, I want pap just like the one you give Martin!" I would pester her constantly because I was jealous of all the attention and wanted her to care for me as she did for Martin. She was always calm and understanding and would patiently take the time to make and feed us both the same food.

My mother would spend hours trying to get Martin to eat something, because he would often end up vomiting. His throat was paralysed, and saliva and food would accumulate and make it difficult for him to swallow properly. She always persevered until he had eaten properly, regardless of the time it took. Mealtimes could easily last longer than an hour, often two.

Although Martin's disabilities could make getting out and about difficult, my parents tried to lead a normal life and arrange as many family activities as they could. My father would often take

Martin out into the community. He would carry him in his arms, as we had no special chair to transport him. He was heavy and awkward, but it was worthwhile, as Martin always enjoyed being outside and around people.

Martin was very used to being close to my family but would not allow any stranger to hold him. If anyone tried, he would stiffen like a stick, pouting and moaning in frustration that would not ease until my mother or father took him back into their arms.

Despite the dark circles of tiredness around my mother's eyes, her work in the house and caring for her family didn't stop her from taking the time each day to play some music on an old gramophone. When the music played, my mother and I would sing and dance to old songs from her great collection of Spanish records from the sixties and seventies. Martin would laugh out loud with joy to see us as we twirled and pranced around the room. Today, I remember those times very fondly. They were sweet and happy moments for all of us.

Years later, when I was better able to understand, my parents told me the story of my brother Martin. At birth, the midwife who helped my mother through labour pulled too hard on his head during the delivery. Doing so caused a stroke that resulted in irreparable damage to his brain and left my mother in a serious state of ill-health. The doctors gave a good prognosis for my mother's recovery, but not such a good one for Martin. He was given just a few months to live.

In those days, the medical staff did not want to take responsibility for any complications, and it seems they took advantage of the youth and naivety of my parents, who were left with a disabled baby who wasn't expected to live for long. The staff offered no explanation, financial compensation or emotional support. My parents had to resign themselves to the situation and try to move forward and do the best they could in unfortunate circumstances. They were very clear that they wanted to give Martin the best care they could for the short time the doctors had given him to live. Even though he had been with them just a few days, they already loved him very much.

Although he had been given only a few months to live, Martin did very well thanks to the absolute dedication of my parents and the constant care and attention of my mother.

"It is a miracle that this child is still alive given his circumstances," the family doctor told my parents three years later. He was surprised to see Martin doing so well considering his serious health problems.

With Martin doing well against the prognosis of the doctors but also requiring so much care and attention, my parents began to worry – especially my mother, who spent most of her day looking after him. Who would be there for Martin if anything were to happen to them?

I was born when Martin was four years old. I was the girl my parents had dreamed of. Of course, my parents now think it was crazy to bring someone into the world to such a burden, but at the time, they only thought of Martin and his well-being. They were also aware that they had not been able to give the necessary care and attention to Lorenzo, and this was becoming evident through his increasingly troublesome behaviour.

I remember perfectly the day that Martin left, never to come back. I was five years old and he was almost ten. When I woke up that morning, I found my parents with tears in their eyes.

"Elisa, Martin has gone to heaven with the little angels," my mother told me while gently sobbing, tears running down her cheeks. I went to his bed, where his body lay still.

"Who am I going to play with now, Martin?" Crying, I said goodbye with a kiss and a hug, knowing that I would not see him again. Deep down, I wasn't sad, because I could sense that he had gone to a place where he would find peace of mind and have freedom from the prison of his body. From that moment, Martin became my guardian angel, and I have always felt the soft feathers of his guidance and protection throughout my life.

Sometimes I think that my life already had a purpose from the moment my parents decided to bring me into the world, and although I couldn't take care of Martin, there would be others like him whom I would have the chance to help throughout my adult life, bringing me great satisfaction and inner peace.

It was the time you spent with your rose
that made it so important.

The Little Prince,
Antoine de Saint-Exupéry

Elisa

A few months after Martin's death, my father found a new job as a carpenter in a large town nearby and the whole family moved to live there. In this big town I spent the rest of my childhood and part of my youth.

If I were to define my childhood in one word, I would say it was bittersweet. I grew up in an affectionate family with good values. My mother and father were hard-working, and although we weren't wealthy and my parents were quite frugal, we never lacked for anything we needed. However, the love and simplicity I experienced as part of my family life was set against a background of bullying and harassment from my peers.

A while after we moved, my mother started working as a shop assistant in a clothing store and my paternal grandmother came to live with us to help look after Lorenzo and me while my parents were working. I really enjoyed having my grandmother at home, because she was like a second mother and helped me fill the void left by Martin's death. Every night I would excitedly ask, "Grandma, tell me a funny story!" as we lay on our beds in my room. She would tell me some of her made-up funny stories and have me in fits of laughter until I would eventually fall asleep, exhausted and smiling.

It didn't take me long to realise that my grandmother didn't know anyone in town and spent many hours alone at home once everyone else had gone to work or school. This worried me, and I came up with the idea of introducing her to a widow who was the grandmother of one of my friends. She lived alone in our street, and I hoped they would be able to keep each other company. From the first moment I introduced them, they liked each other, and a good friendship grew between them. Almost every day they would meet in the afternoon at my house. They would sit in the cosy kitchen drinking coffee with a few drops of anisette, talking and laughing and telling old stories of the past that could last for hours. Most of them would start with "I cannot believe how different life is nowadays. We didn't even have electricity, let alone a television or a washing machine!" Each day they would share different stories of the older times they both knew so well. It made me happy to see them enjoying themselves in each other's company, and I felt able to go outside and play with my neighbourhood friends after school.

Occasionally on Sundays the whole family would go out together, exploring beautiful places in the countryside nearby. We would take a picnic, lay out an old blanket to sit on and enjoy eating all the tasty Spanish food that my mother and grandmother had prepared. Sometimes other family friends would come along, gathering many of the local children together, and we would spend all day laughing and running around in the sunshine.

While I remember many idyllic days, I also suffered bullying for many years by the other children at school. They would make fun of me for my big brown glasses and my sensitive character. My classmates would humiliate me and call me derogatory names that would make me feel terrible anguish and helplessness, leaving me very sad and depressed. I suffered a lot during this time in my life, and I didn't have any support from my parents or other adults.

"That's kid stuff," they would say. "You should laugh at them too or give them a slap."

This was the advice of adults, who dismissed my complaints without giving any more thought to the situation. At first, I tried to put the advice into practice, but I felt very bad doing the same things to them that they did to me. Instead I chose to ignore them and make friends with other children who suffered bullying as well. There was a community of us, a group who were less fortunate or less well off than the others, and we would stay together and have fun amongst ourselves. We were bullied for everything and anything. For wearing glasses, for being taller or shorter, thinner or bigger than average, for growing a little later or earlier than most. All the bullying during my childhood affected my adult life. It created many insecurities and anxieties in my personal relationships but also helped me develop empathy and understanding for vulnerable people.

The only escape I had was my beautiful Cañada, a small village at the foot of the highest mountain of the region, Revolcadores. This was where my family and I used to live with Martin before he died. Although we moved away, my parents kept the house after Martin's death, and almost every weekend, Christmas, Easter and summer holidays we would spend time there. We used to pick fresh flowers from the surrounding meadows and leave them on Martin's tiny white tomb in the small and cosy cemetery where he was buried. Cañada was my liberation from the bullies and somewhere I could find peace of mind. There I would see my cousins and other friends who loved and accepted me just the way I was. During my time in Cañada, we would sometimes head off on excursions to the nearby lake or out on long cycle rides to other beautiful places in the surrounding mountains where we could feel the fresh mountain air and smell the scents of pine, wild rosemary and thyme. We spent the days laughing, jumping and chasing. We would relax around town playing games like tag and hide-and-seek against the backdrop of pines and almond and olive groves, with their long straight rows of trees reaching to the natural plains that stretched out to meet the hills and mountains in the distance.

I would cry every time I had to leave my wonderful Cañada. I would sit in the back of my parents' car with tears on my cheeks as we drove away, back once again to the town that was my personal hell. We would have barely started on our way and I would already be wishing for the week to go by quickly so I could return to Cañada the next weekend.

The freedom I had in my childhood was diminished with the arrival of my youngest brother. Daniel was born when I was almost ten years old after I'd told my parents for many years that I would love to have a sister to play with. My heart fell to the bottom of my stomach when my father exclaimed "It's a boy!" The beautiful face of my little sister dissolved from my mind, but when I saw Daniel's pretty smile, I fell in love in a second, and I knew that I wouldn't change him for anyone. From that point onwards, the rest of my childhood was defined by taking on the responsibilities of a second mother – taking Daniel to school and picking him up after my own classes, feeding him at meal times, showering and dressing him, among many other tasks. Even on weekends, when my parents weren't working, he would come out with my friends and me wherever we went. This was the price I paid for constantly asking my parents to give me a sister to play with. But despite everything, it was worth it, because caring for Daniel and watching out for him created a very strong bond between us, and Daniel and I continue to have a very special relationship today.

> Nostalgia as always had erased bad
> memories and magnified good ones.

> Gabriel García Márquez

My teenage years were an explosion of rebellion after all the responsibilities of my childhood, and I longed for the freedom to become my own person. For a while, my life was full of wild parties where loud music, alcohol, boys and drugs were always present. New experiences came thick and fast – first love, first heartbreak and all the existential depression typical of that age. Luckily, that stormy time faded and allowed sanity and healthier goals to take its place.

Living in a small town had its advantages but also its disadvantages. Life was nice and quiet. Everyone knew each other, and relations between neighbours were generally friendly. There was a good sense of community, and everyone knew what everyone else was up to. The downside was that it felt suffocating. I wanted to break out of small town life and see the world. Visit distant places and experience other ways of life that I knew from the many books that I had read. I had read many, many books. I knew that the only way to get out of my home town and head out into the world was through education. So that was what I did. I spent several years studying for various qualifications and ended up moving to the capital of the region, Murcia.

I gained a higher diploma in administration and finance and ended up working for an estate agent. It was interesting at first but quickly became boring. I was starting to feel lost, and I wondered why I had spent all this time studying. Sure, it had helped me move away from home and see a little more of the world, but I didn't really feel like I was in the right place or doing the right thing with my life. At the same time, I ended up in a romantic relationship that I knew I had no future.

I felt I really hadn't made the right decisions with my studies, my work and my recently broken relationship. I began to feel really low and was wondering what I needed to do to get out of the situation I had got myself into. A friend and flatmate in Murcia called Carmina had finished her nursing assistant studies and found a job as a care assistant in a nursing home in England. I told her, "It's a great opportunity, Carmina, going to England for six months to work as a care assistant while practising English! You will gather the experience you need to work in Spanish hospitals when you return. I wouldn't mind doing something like that to improve my English and to give myself a break, as I really need a fresh start."

Right there and then, Carmina handed me the phone and I called the agency, hoping there would be an opportunity for me to do the same.

To my surprise, the agency contacted me a few days later and offered me a job as a cleaning assistant with accommodation included. Nothing too glamorous, mainly due to my low level of English, but it was the opportunity I was looking for. "I don't mind going as a cleaner. Tell me what papers I have to send you and I'll leave as soon as possible!" I replied enthusiastically. So a few weeks later, I began my new adventure in England without imagining in my remotest thoughts that it would last for many years.

I arrived in England for the first time in early May 2001. Carmina was waiting for me in the arrivals hall of Luton Airport. She was to take me to my new accommodation and workplace in St Albans. However, before getting to meet her, and having just set foot in this new country, I found myself embroiled in my first mess with the language. With my generally clueless nature plus my inexperience travelling by plane and negotiating big airports, I ended up waiting for my suitcase at the wrong carousel. I waited patiently, only coming to realise something was wrong when the carousel was empty and everyone else had left. After an hour of wandering around the huge room, by chance I caught sight of my luggage, circling all alone on a conveyor belt at the back of the room with airport workers standing around it and giving it suspicious looks.

"Is this your luggage? Why did you take so long to pick it up? We were becoming suspicious," one of the attendees asked me in English as I approached to take my suitcase.

"I don't understand anything," I replied, shaking my head in confusion because I couldn't understand a word they said. By pure luck, a Spanish girl who spoke perfect English was walking past and helped me by translating.

"He is asking if this is your suitcase and wondering why it has been hanging around on the belt for so long. They were about to assume it had been forgotten, as it has been here for quite a while."

Oh my gosh! These people will be thinking that it is a bomb! I thought, getting more and more nervous. I explained what had happened, and the Spanish girl translated for the airport workers.

After some more questions and explanations, I was allowed to take my suitcase. I looked towards arrivals out of the corner of my eye as I walked down the hall and saw the airport employees and the Spanish girl staring at me. I could guess from their faces what they were thinking. "This girl is more disoriented and lost than her suitcase." And they were right!

I finally found Carmina in the arrivals hall, wondering where I had got to and starting to get worried. As soon as I had collected my wits about me and calmed down from the stress of the situation, I told her what had happened and we both had a good laugh. Me, smuggling a bomb! Ridiculous!

When I arrived in St Albans, I was amazed to see how beautiful the town was and the luxurious residence where I would spend my next six months. It was a Victorian building, well-kept inside and out. Once inside, I saw it had a very cosy layout with brightly coloured curtains, standard lamps and ornaments, and modern but rustic-style furniture. The residents' rooms were spacious, with their own toilets and decorated to their liking. At the back were large gardens with all kinds and colours of flowers and plants. I imagined the elderly people enjoying pleasant walks and barbecues there in the summer. The only thing that broke the harmony of this apparent sophistication was the strange smell emanating from the carpet – a mixture of urine disguised with floral fresheners, resulting in a stench that would persistently make itself known, just managing to outwit the mind's ability to tune out unpleasant background smells.

I worked hard at my new job, and although I suffered the occasional setback, I felt immensely proud of the experience I was having. For the first time in my life, I felt free. I had left behind the stress and worries of the past and was focusing on a new challenge – English. I hadn't made much progress in six months, mainly because it was easy to get by speaking Spanish with my co-workers. I could engage in some simple chit-chat, the kind of thing everyone learns first – who am I, where do I live, etc. – most of it thanks to the residents of the dementia floor, who kept repeating the same conversations over and over again. But I was still far from fluent.

Caring for the Elderly

Once I had finished my cleaning assistant contract, I went back to Spain. I didn't want to let the little progress I had made learning English go to waste, so I enrolled on an intensive English course. A few years later, and after working a handful of dead-end jobs, I decided I should give myself a second chance at working in England. I had really enjoyed my time in St Albans, so I decided to see if I could get some work there again. With my much-improved English plus the high demand for care workers, I was offered a contract as a care assistant. I delightedly accepted. It would help me improve my English even more, as I would be having a lot of contact with the residents. The care home prepared me for work by providing all the courses required for my new position. Over time, I achieved my diploma in Health and Social Care, specialising in geriatric care and patients with dementia and Alzheimer's disease. While this knowledge prepared me for and gave me an understanding of the technical elements of the job, it was the experiences I had working with and caring for older people almost every day for more than ten years that made me a professional worker and, most importantly, enriched me greatly as a person.

To my surprise, the work, although it was physically and mentally demanding, awoke my humane and compassionate side. I loved the work. It gave me a great sense of warmth and pride to look after those in my care. I would think back and remember my grandparents, and especially my dear paternal grandmother, all of whom had passed away years ago. In some sense, I could share some of my love for my grandparents with the older people I cared for.

"Do you really like this job of cleaning bottoms all the time?" friends and acquaintances would disparagingly enquire about my work.

"Yes. I clean a lot of bottoms for people who aren't able to do it themselves," I would say in response, and I was full of pride.

I never felt more proud of those words than when, years later, after being subjected to two very serious surgical procedures for an intestinal obstruction, I had to be attended to by a care assistant to whom I was tremendously grateful for their professionalism. Not only for their bottom-cleaning skills but also for their moral support.

For me, the job of a care assistant was more than personal assistance and "cleaning bottoms". The tasks depended on the person's circumstances and needs. I would assist with food, medication and other areas where help was needed, always mindful of respecting the autonomy of those needing care as much as possible while motivating them to be as independent as they could be. It wasn't always about such basic essentials, though. We would organise activities and encourage residents to participate – painting, dancing, listening to music, taking walks in the garden – always with the purpose of improving their quality of life.

The moments I enjoyed most were when I got to spend time with the residents during the busy day to just sit and chat – have a joke, make them laugh, listen to their stories and give them a little attention. A small amount of time often seemed to do more good than any amount of medicine.

I will always remember with great affection an old woman with advanced Alzheimer's called Maggie. She was small, with short snow-white hair and large brown glasses that covered much of her petite face. She always wore cheerful colours and would walk through the halls of her floor with a teddy bear in her arms, presenting it as Baby Teddy. This would inspire within me a sense of tenderness.

"Good morning, Maggie. How are you today?" I asked her one day as I brought a cup of tea to her room.

"Today I cannot find myself anywhere," Maggie replied, disoriented.

"Maggie, what a beautiful picture you have with your grandchildren!"
I brought the picture to her from the top of her dresser to distract her a little.

"Who is that old woman in the photo?" she asked, confused, hugging her teddy bear.

"That is you, Maggie. Don't you recognise yourself?" I said innocently.

"Oh! Nooooo! That's not me, that's my grandmother." She laughed, thinking I was joking. She pointed to one of her ten-year-old granddaughters. "This is me," she said, very convinced.

"Oh yes. You look so pretty that I didn't recognise you." I agreed with her, mindful not to upset her reality.

Many of the people I have cared for have marked me with the stories of who they were and what they did in their lives. Over the years, I have heard so many tips and phrases and little pieces of wit and wisdom. Some I still keep with me and do my best to put into practice.

"Enjoy every day to the fullest, because you don't know what tomorrow will bring" or "Life is worth living. It's like a wheel that you have to keep turning and turning every day" – simple refrains that people often overlook, but when given with years of wisdom, the truth in them comes forward. There are many others. "I am soft as water and hard as water." A 97-year-old woman from Hong Kong taught me this old Chinese proverb while doing her routine tai chi exercises in her room. "In the end, it's not the years in your life that count, it's the life in your years." "Eat little, think little and live life with humour," Morris replied, giggling when I asked him about the secret of his longevity. He was ninety-nine years old at the time.

One of the worst things about caring is the moment when it's time to say goodbye forever after having taken care of someone for a long time and getting to know many things about their life. We stay with the person to provide comfort and to make their life as pleasant and dignified as we can during their last moments. I learned to accept loss as part of life, and in some cases, like Maggie, I felt relief when it was time for them to rest after the long and degenerative suffering and loss of identity that the cruel disease of Alzheimer's can bring.

Death is a rest towards the light.

Supporting People With Learning Difficulties

During my early thirties, I suffered a complex and life-threatening illness that resulted in two extremely urgent operations. The second of those was, luckily, successful. The stress of the illness and surgeries left me devastated both physically and emotionally.

After a long period of recovering in Spain, I decided to attempt to pick up the thread of my life once more. I announced to my family that I intended to go back to England to resume my life. My parents accepted my decision with joy and support, although I knew that in their hearts, they wanted to see me settle in Spain. Although they would have preferred me to stay, they were happy to see me starting to get my life back on track after the difficulties and depression I had experienced as I recovered from my illness.

Although in the past I had taken care of older people with dementia and Alzheimer's disease, my illness and my struggle through recovery had given me the desire to feel more connected with my brother Martin. I felt that focusing my efforts on helping people with physical and mental disabilities was truly what I wanted to do with my life.

After several interviews with different organisations, one of them gave me the opportunity I had been hoping for – a job as a support worker for people with learning disabilities. I was to help them and care for them just as I had cared for Martin. Yet, to my surprise and pleasure, it was they who would make me feel loved and valued and give me a purpose in life. I would start once more to wake up every day with a smile on my face.

I loved my work from the beginning. I immediately felt a connection with my co-workers and especially with the people I was supporting. Although my colleagues and I all came from different backgrounds, ages, races, cultures and religions, we all shared the same empathy and compassion for the people we cared for. There was a special bond between us that brought us all together like one big family.

My days were full supporting adults of different ages, genders and races with varying levels of disability, including mild or more acute learning disabilities, autism, Down syndrome, brain injuries and mental health problems. Some lived independently, some in sheltered or supported homes, and others with their families or in dedicated residences.

There are many ways somebody may need assistance that many people take for granted, from day-to-day tasks such as personal grooming and getting dressed to things like taking money from the bank and going shopping – things lots of us do without even thinking about it. Heading into town to take part in your favourite leisure activity can become a struggle without someone to help you navigate public transport, pay the correct fare and interact with others. Visits to the cinema or the theatre, taking a day trip to a favourite place and meeting up with friends can all become a struggle. Helping people achieve these things gives them much more than that experience for a day; it helps them to make friends and to integrate into the community. It brings confidence, happiness and self-worth. Every person I support is a world, and every day is a new challenge, and that made me feel very alive, as I am an active person who really doesn't enjoy a routine life.

The challenges of caring for others are not always as straightforward as helping someone to their local pub for lunch. There were many times I had to face difficult situations where patience and understanding became essential weapons that needed to be used skilfully to help avoid stressful situations – for example, when attending to someone like John, who has behavioural difficulties. Due to his inability to express his emotions verbally, when he is frustrated or angry with someone, he throws things at the people around him and loudly slams the door of his room to get attention. "John, why are you angry?" I would ask when he was going through one of these outbursts. I would hand him a pen and paper and we would began drawing together, supporting the conversation with pictures while I listened and watched to understand his reactions (something that became a unique and personal language once I got to know him) and make sure that I understood his reasons. This would help soothe his anger and take away his feelings of frustration. Once he calmed down, I would suggest that we do some of his favourite activities like drawing, browsing animal magazines or taking a walk in the park. Soon, he would be smiling again.

Occasionally I supported a lady named Rachel, who, due to her learning disability in addition to her autism, would self-harm when she got angry or felt sad, which sometimes caused her serious injury if no one intervened. I remember one day, during the hours I spent supporting her in her own home, Rachel began to repeatedly hit her head hard against the wall. I was worried. I hadn't seen this behaviour from Rachel before.

"Why are you banging your head on the wall, Rachel?" I asked. I was a little scared, not knowing what was behind her behaviour. I could see she would soon hurt herself badly.

"Because I'm so sad," she replied and began shaking, out of control.

"And why are you sad?"

"Jack found a new job and he won't work here anymore." She moved her head back and forth while she spoke and rubbed her hands together with nervous energy.

I understood now what was causing her anxiety. Jack was a support worker whom Rachel was very fond of, and she wouldn't be very happy if he were to leave.

"Yes, Rachel. Jack has found a job closer to where he lives, and it will be more convenient for him, since he won't have to spend so much time driving to work. You should be happy for him. You will still get to see him, because of course he will come to visit from time to time."

"Really?" she replied. "Well, if so, I will write a card to wish him well."

She became calmer once she understood. A simple situation had caused her so much anxiety that she was in danger of harming herself, but in turn, a calm and simple explanation had helped her feel much better. After I took a look at her head to be sure she was fine, she decided to go to her favourite restaurant and after that to see the new version of *Mary Poppins* at the cinema in town. Later on, when we were back at her apartment for the final couple of hours of her support for the day, we began to dance and sing karaoke, singing and laughing our way through some old English songs that she liked so much.

"I had a very happy day thanks to you, Elisa," she said, rubbing her hands vigorously and smiling genuinely.

This made me float so much with happiness that I couldn't feel my feet touching the ground on my walk home. That was the magic of this job: feeling that you had made a difference at the end of someone's day.

As well as organising and helping with activities for individual patients, my colleagues and I also organised events for groups – things like birthday parties, discos, trips to concerts or the theatre, day trips to London and visits to museums. These help the people we support socialise with each other and make friends.

In 2016, another charity group began organising a special sports day during the summer at an outdoor facility in the neighbouring town. The event was set up especially for people with learning disabilities. It was very successful in bringing together a large number of participants from the area. It proved to be very popular and has become a regular thing, running every year since.

Teams of ten people or more participate, generally made up of people living together in the same set of sheltered housing or from the same town. Each team competes against the others to win a participation medal, with the top three teams also winning gold, silver and bronze medals and a small amount of prize money – just enough to treat the team to a meal together. As well as the prizes and the competition, it's also a fun day out for the participants and a great chance for them to get outside and do some healthy exercise with friends.

It was because of these games that I became curious to understand more about the people I supported. I decided to interview some of the participants: Hector, Ron, Arthur, John, Anne and Eric of the Star Team along with Charlotte of the Moon Team. The Star Team participants were the people I supported on a daily basis. I wanted to learn more about them and who they were. By asking them to share their stories, I hoped to find out more about what being involved in the games meant to them and hopefully learn something more about how they coped with their disabilities and health problems. I wanted to go beyond their daily struggles and understand more about their desires, ambitions and passions as human beings.

With prior consent from them and the organisation for which I worked, I arranged a small set of interviews. I hoped to give each team member the opportunity to share a little bit of their story.

Patience is a tree with bitter roots and
very sweet fruits.

Alejandro Jodorowsky

Star House

Star House is a supported living house for people with learning disabilities, where four adults are currently living: Arthur, 45; Ron, 67; John, 73; and Hector, 77. Each has their own private bedroom, and they share communal areas such as the kitchen, the living room, the upstairs bathroom and the garden. They all pitch in to help out with some cleaning tasks according to their preferences. Hector likes to help prepare dinner and do the dishes, Arthur usually sets and clears the table at mealtimes, John likes to empty the bins and Ron sweeps the dining room after dinner and helps with the garden.

They each have their own routine and activities on different days of the week, varying according to the things they enjoy and the assistance they need. They visit the day centre, attend courses, exercise at the local gym, go out for meals and take part in other activities that we plan with them to help them organise their free time.

Every Friday afternoon after dinner, as a group activity, everyone heads out to a disco in a nearby town. It is specially organised for people with learning difficulties, and they all enjoy going. It is a place where they can socialise with other people and have a dance while drinking refreshments and eating snacks. The DJ always plays Hector's favourite song, "The Last Waltz" by Engelbert Humperdinck. Hector loses himself in the joy of the moment and wouldn't change a thing for anyone. Arthur's favourite genre of music is pop. He will spend hours dancing. He repeats his favourite dance non-stop, moving his arms and legs as if he were skiing down a mountain, and thoroughly enjoying himself. Ron will be there with his girlfriend Agnes. They like to have their drinks in a private place, talking with each other for a while and then joining in with everyone else on the main floor. They are a sweet couple and spend their time slow dancing and hugging regardless of the music style, whether it's jump-up-and-down modern beats or some soulful ballad from the eighties. John likes to sit in a quiet area where there are board games to play and puzzles to do. He will work on the puzzles or look at pictures of animals in books while having tea with one of the helpers.

Last year, many parties were organised at home. We had three barbecues in the back garden and several birthday parties. The four residents celebrated their birthdays, inviting their families and friends, and everyone enjoyed abundant party food while having fun dancing and singing along with the karaoke machine. I enjoyed seeing them smile with joy as they opened their gifts – a happy moment that they would remember and chatter about for a whole week.

Most days, Hector, Ron and Arthur have dinner together in the dining room while talking about their day. John prefers to dine quietly in his room after spending all day outside at the day centre, which he attends on Mondays, Tuesdays and Thursdays from 9 a.m. to 4 p.m. After dinner, they sometimes like to sit in the living room and rest, watching television or a movie while having a nice cup of tea. Or perhaps they may prefer to go to their rooms for some privacy. In general, everyone gets along, even if they sometimes have their quarrels, just as in the best families.

Hector

Hector has been living at Star House the longest of all the current residents. Around twenty years ago, the psychiatric hospital where he was a patient closed down. He moved to Star House and has been living there ever since.

Every time a member of staff arrives at Star House, Hector is waiting for them, sitting in his favourite armchair in the lounge waiting to open the door, or sometimes on the bench outside. He greets us in his hoarse and energetic tone. No matter what the time of day, he will say "Good morning! Did you sleep well?" It's hard not to start a shift in a good mood and with a smile on your face after Hector's welcome!

Hector has difficulties communicating due to his learning disability, but he has some phrases – like "Good morning!", "Did you sleep well?", "I am the boss!", "You are a lazy lump!", "Do you work hard?", "Are you going to London today?", "Knock off early!", "Are you Spanish?" and "Jesus loves us, amen!", along with many others – that he manages to use quite well to communicate with the people around him.

He is bald on the top of his head, and the little hair he has on the sides is white with orange flashes, showing that he was a redhead in his youth. Since he doesn't like electric razors, he usually leaves his white beard to grow until it has become so unruly that he has no choice but to go to the local barber for a trim. Behind his golden glasses, his blue eyes twinkle and squint, while his smile is entirely absent of teeth because he doesn't like wearing his dentures.

His mobility is not very good, so he has a walking frame to help him make his way around the house and take short trips outside, and a wheelchair for when the distances are greater. He enjoys the trips in his wheelchair and will bless everyone he meets with one of his special greetings. "Good morning! Did you sleep well? Are you Spanish? Jesus loves you, amen!" This makes people smile and greet him in turn wherever he goes.

Hector has his routines for every day of the week, in which he is accompanied by his support worker. Go to the bank, then food shopping for the week. Attend his courses, or mass on Sundays. But what he likes most is to go to the pub in town at least three times a week, where he eats his favourite dish with a pint of beer or shandy. This is where he enjoys a social life with his old friends and acquaintances. It seems almost everyone there is a friend or acquaintance. He has always lived in the same town, and because of his friendly and charismatic demeanour, Hector is a very popular character.

He almost always takes a taxi into town, since he is more comfortable with that than with taking the bus because of his mobility problems. All the taxi drivers know him by his typical phrase "Are you going to London today?" It makes them smile and adds a bit of interest and character to their day. "I can take you to London now if you want?" some of the taxi drivers will joke with him.

"No today!" Hector will say. "No today! I'm too old! Let's go to the bar!", pointing out the direction he needs to go, which he has come to know very well.

Every time I support Hector, I learn a bit more about his past and the challenges that he has been through. One day, during his hours of support, we were sitting at the bar as usual. Hector was eating his fish and chips and drinking his pint of beer when an old friend of his approached the table and asked if he could sit with us to chat for a while.

"Yes, Jim, sit down!" Hector said with a friendly wave and pointed out a chair at our table.

Jim, despite his mild mental disability, can express himself quite well, and he told me that he knew Hector from the psychiatric hospital where they were patients for many years. During the time he spent with us, he told me a little bit about how things used to be.

"I am very happy to live in my own apartment outside the hospital," Jim told Hector.

"We work hard, eh, Jim!" Hector commented in his loud voice.

"Hector handed out meals and bottles of milk to hospital companions at mealtimes. He worked hard in those days."

"A lot of scrubbing!" Hector gestured like he was scrubbing at some imaginary surface.

"We also used to work at the hospital farm nearby, planting some vegetables, and Hector used to sit down to have a rest when no one was looking at him. You were a lazy lump!" Jim said, laughing out loud, making Hector laugh as well.

"Lazy lump!" Hector chuckled.

After the conversation with Jim, I did a little research on the internet to find out some information about the psychiatric hospital where they had spent time together.

People with learning disabilities lived in wards placed on either side of the central drive, with approximately thirty residents downstairs and dormitory sleeping upstairs. There were few single rooms. The normal dress for residents was loose-fitting uniforms and hospital-provided underwear. Meals were prepared and cooked in a central kitchen on the site before distribution to the wards in heated trolleys. As a result, the food was not very fresh or appetising when presented to the residents. There was little opportunity for privacy and a strict daily routine, which included some day activities in centres away from the ward. In summary, it seems that all psychiatric hospitals at the time held standards of care and accommodation that would be considered far from satisfactory today. There were many institutional practices that viewed residents as a group rather than as individuals.

Reading about the hospital, I didn't get a great impression of how things were back then, but I guess at that time it was what society thought was best, and the hospital was the most suitable place for people like Jim and Hector to live. It helped me to understand better why Hector still had certain habits, such as sleeping with his wallet in his pyjama pocket or hiding food under his pillow to eat at night, as well as his anxiety and the controlling behaviour he showed on some occasions towards the workers and his housemates.

After the closure of the psychiatric hospital, the patients were moved to various independent or supervised houses and flats, allowing them to live independently and integrate into the community. This was a great improvement in their quality of life.

Hector occasionally likes to go to mass on Sunday mornings at a local Catholic church. He was an altar boy there in his childhood, and the pastor has known him for a very long time. Hector always shows great respect during mass by remaining silent during the service, which is very unusual for him. During the service, he will open the Bible that he keeps in his trolley — most of the time upside down — and pretend he is reading at the same time as the priest reads the sermon. At the end of each prayer, he shouts an energetic "Amen!" that reverberates around the church and surprises some of the other parishioners!

One day, after mass, the priest, glad to see Hector, approached and greeted him.

"Good morning, Hector. It's an honour to see you here."

"Good morning, Father! Are you Spanish?" Hector returned the greeting in his typical sharp and hoarse voice. "I am the boss!" he said, pointing at himself.

"I have known you are the boss for a long time, Hector. Since you were a young boy." The priest nodded with a smile.

"Get a haircut!" Hector exclaimed.

"I wish I could have one." The priest brought both hands to his bald head. All of us nearby, including the priest, were tickled with laughter at Hector's joke.

"Jesus loves us, *amen*!" said Hector.

"Amen! I hope you keep well, and I'll see you around," the priest said in farewell.

Hector's sister Joanne and his niece Lauren are very important to him. They come to visit him or call him on the phone every week. His sister told me that Hector was born without any difficulties and was quite a healthy baby, but at the age of four, he suffered an attack of meningitis that damaged his brain and caused serious mental disability as a result.

Hector has a girlfriend named Catherine, though he calls her by the nickname Cathy. They both lived at the psychiatric hospital, but they didn't see each other for a long time after it closed down. They started dating a couple of years ago after meeting by chance at Hector's favourite bar. Upon meeting, their conversation began in a familiar and straightforward way.

"Good morning, Cathy! Did you sleep well?"

"Yes, Hector, like a lemon," Cathy replied.

And with that, they went on to spend their time sharing stories of the old days when they used to share cigarettes in the hospital garden and joke around together on the ward. Watching them together, it was easy to see they were very good friends and had a lot of affection for each other. From that day onward, they decided that they wanted to meet regularly every Friday to have lunch together and chat for a while.

Catherine is a few years younger than Hector. She has some communication problems and it can be difficult to understand what she says. This can be difficult for her, as she can become very anxious when asked to repeat what she has said so that people can understand. Her hair is grey, and she likes to wear it short. She wears glasses, and her smile reveals the few teeth that still remain. She is small, with a slight limp that is aggravated throughout the day by her arthritis, so she always takes the arm of her assistant while moving around. "Hector, behave!" Catherine will admonish Hector when he is talking a lot. Hector will listen and stop talking, but never for much longer than a handful of minutes. She may tell him off occasionally for talking too much, for repeating himself over and over or for asking silly questions, but when it comes to their goodbyes, she is always affectionate. "You are a good boy, Hector. See you next Friday!" she will say and plant a little kiss on his cheek, leaving Hector all bashful and flushing red, wearing a big grin on his face.

In general, while Hector's relationship with his housemates is good, he is most strongly attached to Arthur. Together they will prepare tea and settle down to watch television and films after dinner. They like to go together to watch the local football games at the pitch nearby. Hector worries when Arthur is away from home for a long time, and he sits on the bench at the entrance to the house and waits for him to return. "Arthur, come on! Come now!" he mutters anxiously under his breath, and he won't stop until he sees Arthur's familiar face coming down the road.

One afternoon after dinner, Hector and I were sitting at the dining room table and I asked if he would like to tell me things about himself and his life. He was delighted to do so. I asked some simple questions that he would be able to understand and answer in his own way.

"Well, Hector, to start, I want to thank you for helping me prepare dinner, even if you do cut the potatoes and carrots finer than a razor blade and use half a bottle of washing-up liquid to scrub the dishes!"

"Do we work hard, eh, Elisa?" he said, twisting his fingers through his unruly beard.

"Yes, Hector, you always work hard."

He smiled broadly at the praise. "What do we have for dinner tomorrow?" he asked. I showed him the menu stuck to the fridge and pointed at the photo of the dish we would be making tomorrow. Shepherd's pie. "Shepherd pie, I like it!" he said, licking his lips.

"It's your favourite food, but you also like other things, right?"

"Yes. Shepherded pie, fish and chips, beef stewed, mmmmm," he said, twiddling his beard as he tried to remember some more. "And apple pie!"

"What about kippers?" I added jokingly because I know he hates them.

"Stink!" he exclaimed, pinching his nose with a look of disgust on his face.

"So, Hector. Let me know a little bit about yourself. Tell me about your family."

"My parents and Maurine are in heaven. They are not here anymore. It's very sad, Elisa." As he spoke, he raised both arms and looked up towards the ceiling. Maurine was his sister.

"Who are the most important people for you now?"

"Joanne, Lauren, Lassie and the queen. *Aaamennn!*"

"Who is Lassie?"

"Lauren's dog. She barks when she is hungry. Woof! Woof! Do you have a dog?" Hector asked.

Hector would ask every member of staff and many people he met if they had a dog, generally right after asking them if they were Spanish. Whenever anyone replied "yes", his next question was always "Does it bark?"

"I don't have a dog, although I love them a lot. Perhaps in the future I will adopt a rescue dog or a cat, as I love animals. Do you like animals, Hector? I know you enjoy it when Melvin brings Georgia and Karma to the house on Wednesdays."

"Yes! Good dogs."

"You also enjoy going to the zoo, I think."

"Yes. I went yesterday with Amanda to the zoo, and I saw you there, Elisa!"

"You saw me there?" I said, surprised.

"Yes. I saw a lot of monkeys !" He giggled and slapped the sides of the chair.

"Oh ho! You're the cheeky monkey! So, who is your best friend?"

"Arthur," he answered without hesitation.

"Why Arthur?"

"He makes me tea and we watch movies and the Hammers. Up the Hammers!"

The Hammers was a local football team. Hector enjoyed watching football and would enthusiastically cheer for the Hammers regardless of who was actually playing.

"What is your favourite colour?"

"Blue!" he said, pointing to the red colour of a magazine in front of him.

"But, Hector, that's red!"

"Yes. Red!"

"Tell me about your girlfriend."

"Yes. Cathy."

"Where did you meet her?"

"Hospital."

"Did you used to live in the same hospital?"

"Yes."

"Cathy told me that you both used to go to the garden and smoke a cigarette together while you were having a chat. Did you like her then?"

He gave a nervous laugh and then suddenly pointed to a tree branch through the dining room window. "Elisa, I saw a bird!"

"Hector, Hector! You are very cunning."

He made me laugh as he changed the subject, a little flush of red on his cheeks. "Are you Spanish?" he asked.

"Yes, I am Spanish, and this time you are correct, even if you ask everyone the same thing. Why do you ask everyone if they are Spanish? Were all the nurses in the hospital where you lived Spanish?"

"Hola! Hola! Hola, Miss Elisa."

He surprised me with a fluent Spanish accent, making me laugh again. "What is your favourite sport?"

"Boxing. I'm a boxer," he said, showing me his skinny arms and his non-existent muscles, though for him, they were vigorous and strong.

"Ah! I see that you are fit for this year's sports day."

"Yes! We're going to win this year." He said this seriously, convinced of this self-evident truth.

"What game do you like best on sports day?"

"Basketball!" He pretended to throw a ball.

"Throw the balls into the basket. And what about the javelin and the hoops? You were also very good at those last year."

"I am the boss." He smiled proudly as he ran his fingers through his beard.

"What day-to-day activities do you enjoy most, Hector?"

"Pub. Beer. Boxing. Disco." He furrowed his brow, thinking. "Umm, and Christmas!"

"What is special for you at Christmas?"

He leaned forward in the chair and looked very serious as he replied, "Christmas pudding!"

"Would you like to go on vacation somewhere nice this year?" I asked, though I knew Hector didn't like sleeping away from home.

"No. I'm very old."

"Tell me, how old are you?"

"Forty," he responded confidently.

"Only forty? I think you are hiding a few years up your sleeve!"

He scratched his head. "Seventy?"

"Well, that's closer, but you're still hiding a few years, because according to your birth date, you are seventy-seven!"

Hector began to stroke his beard again and seemed a little confused. "Very old, Elisa." He laughed.

"What is your dream come true?" I asked.

"London!"

"Shall we plan another day trip to London and another to Brighton to see the sea and the ships like we did last month?"

"Yes! London train and bus, Elisa."

"Of course, and we can have a beer and fish and chips in the pub near Buckingham Palace. Perhaps you will see the queen!" I joked with him, as I know he adores the queen. He has many photos of her around his room.

"Haha! The queen! You are a lovely lady, Elisa." He said this in a very sincere tone, and even though he said the same thing to all the female staff, he made me feel special.

"Oh! Thank you, Hector. You are one in a million, and I really mean it."

"Yes. I am the boss!" He pointed both of his hands to his chest.

"Well, Hector, thank you very much for our lovely chat. To end our conversation, I would love for you to do one of your special blessings."

"Yes, Elisa." Hector gestured to the cross as he called out, "Father and son and the bloody spirit!"

"Holy, Hector! The Holy Spirit!"

"Aaamennn!" he said powerfully and gestured to the cross once more.

Just then, Arthur entered and asked Hector if he wanted a cup of tea. Hector nodded without hesitation and stood up quickly from the dining table and headed into the living room, where he and Arthur would watch television together every night.

"Knock off early, Elisa," he said.

And with that, the conversation was ended.

Arthur

Arthur is the youngest in the house at forty-five, and all of his housemates appreciate and respect him for his noble character. He is tall and robust, but despite having a strong appearance, there is an innocent look behind his large dark blue eyes. His hair is light brown with a little grey through his sideburns, and he has a small bald spot on his crown that gives him a look reminiscent of a friar.

In addition to his mild learning disability, Arthur is also autistic. His character is gentle, and he never gets angry with anything or anyone. He is always calm and listens to the advice that the support workers give him. "Arthur, eating all six doughnuts in the package is not healthy because they contain a lot of sugar and fat," or "Putting half a pot of ketchup on the sausages can make your stomach ache," or "You will be far too hot wearing your winter jacket, scarf, hat and gloves outside in the thirty-degree heat today." Advice that he will put into practice when he is in front of us, but when he is alone, he will give in to his whims, eating all the doughnuts and using up all the ketchup.

Arthur came to live at Star House nearly four years ago with his father, Harry. They were very close. Harry also had a mild learning disability, and he died from a heart attack a year after moving into the house, leaving Arthur very affected by his sudden loss. It was thanks to the moral support of his housemates and the care staff that he was able to resume a normal life after a few months of depression.

After the death of his father, Arthur became very close to Hector despite their constant quarrels.

"Hector, with that beard, you look like Santa Claus!" Arthur tells Hector sometimes to goad him.

"Leave me alone, Arthur!" Hector will say angrily, leaving to go to his room. Minutes later, Arthur will prepare a cup of tea for Hector and another for himself. Hector will come back from his room and they will be back to being friends as always.

As soon as the support workers enter the house and after Hector's exuberant welcome, Arthur is the one who keeps us up to date with the news from the television, the gossip of the house and the latest film he has seen at the cinema, with much enthusiasm and in great detail.

"Do you know that Notre Dame Cathedral is on fire? Do you know that Brexit has been postponed for a few more months? Teresa May has resigned! I've seen it this morning on the news. Ah! Amanda has called this morning and says she is sick and an agency assistant is coming to cover her position today. Do you know that they are going to release the *Chucky 8* movie next year?"

One Wednesday, after eating a healthy meal of roast chicken salad with avocado and a yogurt, a recipe he had learned to make on his eating healthy course, Arthur decided to go to the pub to play some pool and darts. He won almost every game and felt very proud of himself, as he had improved a lot since he had started practising a few months earlier. After playing pool, we sat down on the big comfy chairs, enjoying the atmosphere, listening to the background music and drinking some refreshment. He began to tell me in detail about a movie that he had recently seen.

"I really liked the new version of Star Wars. It has very good special effects, but the characters are not the same as in the original," he explained.

"Oh, sure. The characters in the original movie must be very old," I said.
I hadn't yet seen the latest Star Wars film. Nor any of the older ones. I must be the only person on the planet who hasn't seen them.

I asked him, "What kind of movies do you prefer, Arthur?"

"I really like science fiction and superhero action movies where the goodies shoot the baddies. Bang! Bang! I also like thrillers, horror and comedies."

"What is your favourite movie ever?"

"I have many favourite movies, Elisa." He paused, took another sip of his drink and continued excitedly. "I like all the movies of Star Wars, all the Halloween movies, Spiderman, Batman, Dracula, the devilish doll Chucky, Frankenstein and lots of others that I don't remember now." He was rubbing his hands with excitement at talking about his favourite subject – the cinema.

"I'm not surprised you don't remember them all. You must have seen all the movies there are to see! There aren't even any movies in the cinema right now that you haven't seen before."

"Oh yes, there will be soon! Next week, two new films come out: *Tolkien* and *Rocketman.*"

"Did you used to go to the movies often before you moved to Star House?"

"When I lived at my uncle's house, I used to watch films on television and only went to the movies on special occasions. Now I go two or three times a week." He gestured with his hands as he was talking.

"How long have you been living in Star House?"

"I've been living in Star House for four years now. My father moved with me but died three years ago of a heart attack," he said sadly and bowed his head.

"Where did you live before moving to Star House?"

"I lived with my father in my uncle's house in the nearby town."

"Are you still in touch with your uncles or your mother?"

"I don't have contact with any of them."

"Oh. Why not?"

"Mum left my dad and me when I was little. She has another family now. I prefer not to talk about it, please, Elisa." With this he became a little overwhelmed and began to move his head from side to side nervously.

"Who is your best friend in the house?" I changed the subject, as I could see he was upset.

"I get along with everyone, but I'm most attached to Hector. We both like watching TV shows or movies after dinner. We also like to go to football matches on Saturdays at the local pub and the park next to the house when they are in season."

"Who is your best friend outside the house?"

"Anne. We sometimes go to Morrisons to have lunch together on Saturdays," he replied with a big smile on his face.

"What a big smile. Do you like Anne?" I teased him.

"She's very pretty. But we are just friends." He looked away and twisted his fingers together as he said Anne was pretty.

"Would you like to find a girlfriend, Arthur?"

"Yes. I want to go to speed dating the next time the day centre organises another event. In the last one, Ron found his girlfriend Agnes, but I didn't find anyone that I liked. Maybe next time I will have more luck." He sighed.

"What activities do you like to do during the week?"

Arthur stopped for a moment to think and said, "I go to an arts and crafts course on Monday mornings, on Tuesdays I go to the bank and do my food shopping, on Fridays and Sundays I go to the cinema. On Wednesdays I go to the Eating Healthy course, where we cook healthy recipes that help regulate my cholesterol. I recently finished a course to learn how to handle money, and now I have started a new course to learn to read and write. Support workers also help me during my support hours." He gestured a lot with his hands while explaining.

"Do you think you are advancing with your learning?"

"I'm learning the alphabet, and I already know how to write it." He smiled at this, very pleased with his progress. I took some paper and a pen from my bag and wrote out the alphabet for Arthur to copy. He spoke the letters out loud and copied them underneath where I had written them.

"Very well done, Arthur! You write them neater than I do."

"I need more practice and then I'll start learning to spell words and write them. My teacher Ben says it's a matter of practice and time."

"Any other activity you like?" I asked.

"I go to the gym almost every day at seven in the morning, and that helps me to be fit and keep my weight down. I have lost more than twenty kilos, you know." He rubbed his belly.

"That's great! I see you are getting very fit for this year's sports games."

"Yes, Elisa. We still don't know what day they are going to celebrate this year. We are waiting for the organisation to tell us the day. Do you know if Matthew and Catherine will join the team this time? We will work hard to win a prise. This year I would like to participate in the speed, relay and obstacle course, as I feel more agile than last year after the kilos I have lost." Arthur was very proud of the weight he had lost attending the gym. "And I really enjoyed the party at the end and the cakes and drinks we were given."

"Arthur! You are always thinking about food! What do you like most about living in Star House?"

"I really like living in Star House. I have my own key, and I can leave and enter the house whenever I want. I go to the cinema twice a week and make my own purchases; I also go by myself to a comedy club at the pub some Tuesday evenings. I'm happy with the workers and my housemates." He stopped to think and added, "Ah! And I have my room decorated in red with carpet and posters of my favourite Marvel superheroes."

"Is red your favourite colour?"

"Yes, red," he replied without hesitation, pointing to the sweater he was wearing.

"Why?"

"I just like it very much. This is my favourite jumper and it's red. I like it!"

He was humming along to the background music, so I asked him, "What is your favourite music?"

"I have many favourites. I like the music of the eighties and nineties. Like the music we are listening to now. Kylie Minogue, Jason Donovan, Abba, Michael Jackson, Spice Girls, Steps."

He stopped the conversation for a moment and listened to the song that was playing on the jukebox, "Barbie Girl" by Aqua, and then he suddenly stood up to dance to it enthusiastically. Once the song finished, he sat down, and I continued.

"When was your last holiday?"

"Last year, I went on my first vacation to Great Yarmouth for five days. Tendai organised everything for me." He rubbed his hands together vigorously. "He's also organising another holiday for ten days to Disneyland in Paris by the end of this year!" He rubbed his hands together some more.

"What are your plans for the future, Arthur?"

He narrowed his eyes, thinking about the answer. "Uhmm, learn to read and write well, my trip to Disneyland Paris, sports games, Christmas and find a girlfriend."

"Tell me a funny joke."

"Knock, knock! Who is? Doctor Who with an electric screwdriver! Knock, knock! Who is? It's Batman in the washing machine." He clutched his stomach and bent over, pretending to laugh, very amused by his nonsensical jokes.

"Look at the time! And we still have to do your food shopping and go back home for dinner. Amanda is preparing a delicious shepherd's pie and apple crumble for dessert."

We had stayed out chatting for longer than we'd expected. On hearing the word "food", he got up as quick as lightning and strode directly to the front door.

"Let's go, Elisa! I don't want to miss dinner."

Ron

Ron has been living at Star House for three years. He moved to the house after social services found him living alone in his parental home, isolated and neglected. In the beginning, he found it difficult to get used to the idea of sharing a house with other people, as he had lived alone for so long, but he soon adapted perfectly to his new life with his housemates. Ron requires a greater level of support and personal care than his housemates due to his many mental and physical health problems, and this means he has a helper with him for almost the whole day. The time we spend with him is very rewarding, as he is full of life and has the ability to enjoy the small things from day to day. This makes a big difference to his mood and quality of life in general.

Ron is a very joyful person with a good sense of humour and a great ability to express himself and tell jokes when he is happy. He is bald, of medium height and somewhat plump. He often smiles, and when he does, his cheeks show small dimples. He loves to spend time gardening, cutting dead branches from the trees and planting flowers and vegetables when the weather allows. He also enjoys music. He goes every Thursday to a music course, where he sings and dances and plays the guitar. The staff find it curious that after almost every lesson he comes home missing a string from his guitar – a big mystery for us, as they can never be found, not in his bags and not in Star House or anywhere at his music course. He is also interested in many other activities, such as going to the cinema, bowling, pool, darts and karaoke, and he always attends any social activities or parties that he is invited to.

One afternoon, after his apple pie made from the fruit he had collected himself from the house apple tree, we sat in the garden to enjoy the sunny weather and have a chat. I had one cup of tea while Ron had two together, just as he liked it.

"Would you like to tell me something about the story of your life, Ron?" I asked him, curious to know more about his past.

"Oh! Yes, I would love to, Miss Elisa," Ron replied with enthusiasm.

"So, tell me a little about your family and your childhood."

He settled back into his chair, took a sip of his tea and began his story. "I was born in a small town in the province of Hertfordshire. My mother was a housewife and my father was a farmer. I have four brothers and two sisters." He stopped for a moment as he remembered and then continued. "I went to the village school until I was eleven, when my father found a new job in a nearby town. My family and I moved there, where I continued school until fifteen. Shortly after, I started working as a farmer at the local farm, and this was my job until I had an accident."

He paused for a sip of tea and then continued his story. "When I was sixteen years old, while driving a tractor through the countryside in an isolated area of the farm, the tractor fell into a ditch full of water and mud and I became trapped underneath with water up to my neck. I was trapped there for a long time until I was discovered and rescued. I can't remember how many hours or days I was there, but it felt like an eternity. It was horrible, Elisa!" he said with a sad expression, looking down at the table.

After a short silence, he continued. "I spent a lot of time in the hospital, during which I was diagnosed with mental problems." (Ron has schizophrenia and bipolar depression.) "From there, I was transferred to a psychiatric hospital, where I lived for many years, though I can't remember how many." He closed his eyes, trying to remember. "Years later, I was discharged, and I went to live with my mother, who lived alone after the death of my father. I lived with her for many years until she died." I could see the sadness in his eyes as he took another sip of his tea. "After the death of my mother, I lived alone for a long time. I was feeling empty inside and my life was meaningless. I only had the energy to eat and sleep."

At that time, Ron developed an eating disorder that he controls today under medical supervision and with the assistance of the support workers. We try to keep him busy during the day with activities he enjoys. This helps to prevent him from spending the day eating compulsively.

"Do you have good memories of your childhood?" I encouraged him to relate something positive.

"I had a beautiful childhood. My brothers and I used to play together in the fields. We also fought, but I think that's normal between brothers, isn't it? In general, we all had a good relationship, and I really enjoyed being part of a big family."

"Are you still in contact with any of your brothers today?"

"Yes. I get along with everyone, but I have a close relationship with my brother Roger and my sister Mary. We call each other frequently. I have another sister in Australia with whom I speak on the phone sometimes. Years ago, before my unfortunate incident, I went to visit her in Australia and I had a great time. I saw kangaroos and koalas!" He raised the sleeve of his shirt, showing me a tattoo of a koala on his arm that he had had done during his stay and of which he is very proud.

"Are you happy to live here at Star House?"

"Yes. Although sometimes I have disagreements with John because he doesn't like me. Nearly every time he sees me, he throws his glasses at my head! It's hard to live with people after living alone for so long. You know, Elisa, I would like to have my own house."

"Who is your best friend in the house?"

"Ummm, let me think. Arthur and Hector. I enjoy our chat at dinner time."

"What are your interests and hobbies?"

"I like working in the garden. Have you seen my mini vegetable plot? I have planted cabbages, carrots, tomatoes, potatoes and parsley. Come and I will show it to you."

He was excited to show me and eagerly got up from the chair and led me to the fenced area at the bottom of the garden where he had his small plot. He began proudly pointing out each of his vegetables and herbs.

"That's great, Ron. So we can cook with some organic vegetables."

"The cherry tomatoes can almost be eaten." He pointed to the tomato plants, where the small green tomatoes were visible between the leaves. After showing me his vegetable garden, we walked back to the chairs and sat back down, and I asked him some more questions.

"Apart from the garden and your mini allotment, what other hobbies do you have?"

"I also like to go to the movies and listen to music, and I enjoy arts and crafts. I go to a music course and a painting course. I really like going to the disco on Friday afternoons, you know? There I stay with my girlfriend Agnes while we have a drink together and then dance to some catchy music!"

"I have already noticed that you like to dress up on Fridays."

"Of course. I like to look elegant for Agnes. My favourite outfit is my jeans with the blue dotted shirt and my leather jacket."

"Tell me about your girlfriend Agnes. Where did you meet her?"

"Oh! My dear Agnes. I met her two years ago at a speed dating event organised by the day centre I usually go to." He stopped to think for a moment before continuing. "We have been very happy together since that day, and we almost always give each other gifts when we meet."

"I do remember the day you bought a box of chocolates."

"Yes! I remember. I ended up eating them all during the journey before giving them to Agnes, but I was very hungry, you know?" He looked a little downhearted at making an excuse for eating the chocolates.

"At least you left her three!"

"Well! Three is better than none, right?" he said, and we both laughed. "We are officially engaged, do you know, Elisa? We want to get married soon, move to a big house and have a lot of children." He told me this in a serious tone, believing what he was saying.

"Maybe it is a little late for children?" I mentioned this because Ron and Agnes are both almost seventy years old.

"Uhmmm" – he scratched his head – "you're right!" he said thoughtfully. "Well then, we can start the family with a dog and a cat, you know?" He laughed out loud again. Ron has an infectious laugh, and I couldn't help laughing along with him.

"What was the last movie you saw at the cinema?"

"*Night School*. A very funny movie, Elisa."

"I hope you didn't fall asleep in the middle of the movie like you did the last time I accompanied you to the cinema, remember?"

It was a very funny situation, because Ron fell deeply asleep, and in one of the scenes of the movie, somebody was knocking loudly on a door. Ron woke up with a start, suddenly disoriented, and started saying, "Who is it? Who is it?" while looking back and forth. "Come in! Come in!" This set myself and the people around us giggling.

"Yes, that was really funny, but this time I did not fall asleep," he said seriously.

"Tell me, Ron, what do you think you are good at?"

"Gardening and flirting with women," he replied with a mischievous expression. "I like to flirt, but the one I really love is my Agnes."

"What activities have you enjoyed most this year?"

"My holidays in Blackpool were great, you know, Elisa? Super cool! Kelly, my key worker, organised them for me. I would like to go next year to another romantic place near the seaside with my fiancée Agnes." He paused for a moment. "Ah, last week I spent a day in London with Alex. I travelled by train and took buses around London. I rode for the first time on the London Eye. Amaaaazing views!" He rubbed his hands with excitement as he remembered.

"Are you going to participate in the sports games this year?"

"Of course. Do you know when it will be held this year?"

"Sometime around September, but I don't know the exact day. When the time approaches, the organisation will send me an email with the date and all the information. I will let the team know so we can make all the arrangements."

"Please, Elisa, do it! I'm looking forward to the day. Last year we had a lot of fun even though we didn't win anything. This year our Star Team is hoping to be in one of the top three positions. Every day I walk to the supermarket to buy fresh milk and then I walk around the neighbourhood to get some exercise so I can be more agile in the tests."

"That's great, Ron. Do you also count the hours of dancing at the disco as training?" I was kidding.

"Sure. I'm the king of the dance floor!" he said, waving his arms, pretending to dance. "At the games there is also a dance choreography test that I was very good at last year."

"And at the party after the event last year, you also did well, as you didn't stop dancing, which was a good thing, as you had spent a lot of time eating!"

"Yes. I had a great time. It was a fun party. Ah! Do you know which colour our team T-shirts will be this year? Last year we had green."

"I don't have a clue. We'll have to wait and see. What colour would you like this year?"

"Red – red or blue."

"Are those your favourite colours?"

"Yes, Miss Elisa, and I also like yellow."

"Okay, well, I'll see what I can do. Perhaps I can ask the organisers to make our shirts in red. Tell me, what is your favourite song?"

"'Bridge over Troubled Water' by Simon and Garfunkel." He began to sing the song passionately with his eyes closed. "... troubled water, ummm, troubled trouble ..."

"What goals do you have in your life, Ron?" I asked him after a while.

"Marry my beloved Agnes and move to our own house." He thought for a few moments and added, "Although the boyfriend life is not too bad without so much commitment." He began to laugh, again revealing his mischievous dimples.

"What do you think you would be doing now if you were still living alone in your parents' house?"

"Probably nothing, Elisa. Eat and sleep," he said in a sad voice and looked down at the floor.

"Don't be sad, Ron. Tell me one of your funny jokes as we finish our chat. It is getting quite late."

"Jack and Jill went up to the hill, Jill farted and sent Jack away!"

"Ron!" I laughed. "You can be very silly sometimes."

"With your permission, Elisa," he said with a yawn, "I am going to make my cups of tea and then head up to my room to watch a movie and to rest, because early tomorrow I am going on an excursion to Southend-on-Sea with people from the day centre."

"Okay. I will be with you shortly to help you get ready for bed."

Ron headed to the kitchen to prepare his two cups of tea. As he was making the teas, I could hear him singing "Troubled water ... troubled! Troubled ..." Ron was a surprisingly good singer and would always sing with all his heart.

John

Before moving to Star House almost eight years ago, John had lived most of his life with his parents, his sister Brenda, and his brother Paul. All three siblings have some degree of learning difficulty, with John's being the most severe. When his parents died, his brother was transferred to a supported living residence and John stayed for a while living with his sister Brenda. Eventually his disability and the care he required became too great a burden for her, so the social services moved John to Star House, where he has been living ever since.

John is a man of medium height, thin and agile. His face is long. He has grey hair and wears strong glasses to correct his poor vision. He has communication difficulties, but since living at Star House, his communication has improved a lot and he can sometimes say well-coordinated short phrases like "Arthur is my friend," "I like dogs," "I like Amanda's car" or "I like Gemma."

John is often frustrated when he cannot communicate what he feels or when he is in a crowded place. When there are too many people around and the noise gets too loud, he will start swearing and banging on doors or throwing things at people or onto the floor. To avoid these changes in his behaviour, the assistants supporting him will motivate him to do relaxing activities that he enjoys, and hopefully this will calm him and help him to avoid getting stressed.

He has activities scheduled on weekdays. On Mondays, Tuesdays and Thursdays he goes to a day centre from nine in the morning to four in the afternoon, where the participants do different things such as arts and crafts, painting, cooking, music and going on excursions. On Wednesdays, he often has lunch in a quiet restaurant in town with his sister Brenda, with the support of a helper to make it possible. On Friday mornings, he does his banking and usually his weekly food shopping, accompanied by his key worker, Gemma. She is responsible for monitoring his general health and helping him attend doctor's appointments, check-ups, eye tests and anything else he needs. Gemma also helps him to organise his annual vacation with Brenda.

On Friday afternoons, he likes to go with his housemates to the disco, where he usually sits in a quiet corner with one of the support workers, assembling a jigsaw puzzle or looking at an animal magazine while drinking a cup of tea. At the weekend, John loves going to the zoo, walking in the park or just relaxing in his room listening to his favourite music and sometimes taking a nap.

Almost every evening after showering and putting on his pyjamas, John likes to come to the office to sit and draw while the support workers perform administrative tasks. One day, he arrived while I was updating some records.

"Did you go to lunch with your sister Brenda today?" I asked.

"Yes! Yes! Brenda! Brenda!" He smiled openly, revealing a jagged tooth.

"You love your sister very much, don't you?"

"Yes! Yes! Much! Much!" He kissed the palm of his hand and blew the kiss into the air. "Brenda! Brenda!"

"Did you have your favourite for lunch?"

"Uhmmm, fish and chips! Chips! Chips! Yumm mmm!"

"John, would you like to tell me something about yourself?"

"Yes! Yes!" John smiled and nodded.

"What is your favourite colour?"

With this, I put in front of him a box of markers containing many pens of different colours, and he selected the blue one, repeating aloud, "Blue! Blue!"

"What is your favourite toy?"

He produced several handfuls of miniature cars, lorries and tractors from his pocket and piled them onto the table. Just a few of them – say ten or twenty! He picked one and held it up. "Car! Car!" Then from his other pocket he brought out a small collection of wristwatches. "Broken! Broken!"

"How can they be broken? You just bought a new wristwatch a few days ago."

He smiled. "Yes. Buy a watch. New one! New one!"

This was one of John's hobbies. Each Saturday at the market, he loved to go and look at the old watch stall. There were many different watches on display, some for ladies, some for men. Some big flashy expensive ones. But John's favourites were the ones kept in the big old box at one end of the stall. He would spend a long time digging through the collection of cheap old second-hand watches until he found one that caught his eye, and we would help him buy it. Although old, they often worked well enough. Well enough until John got them home, where he would immediately begin dismantling them!

I showed John a photo of him and Georgia, a dog that he adores. Once a week, a retired gentleman called Melvin brings two adopted puppies called Georgia and Karma to visit the residents as therapy. It is intended for the people we support, but in reality it is a great therapy for all of us, as it helps us break away from the daily routine. Everyone enjoys the dogs' company, stroking them and playing with them. It's a lovely day when the puppies visit, and it leaves everyone with smiles on their faces.

John gave the photo little kisses, saying, "I love you, doggy."

"Who is your best friend from the house?"

"Arthur! Arthur is my best friend," he said, smiling.

"And outside the house?"

"Marc! Marc! Marc!" Marc is a friend from the day centre John visits.

"What is your favourite music?"

John left the office, went up to his room and returned bringing three CDs, one by The Shadows, one by Buddy Holly and the other by Elvis Presley.

"Do you like Buddy Holly?"

"Yes! Yes! Peggy Sue!" He kissed the Buddy Holly CD.

"Do you like going to the disco on Fridays with your housemates?"

"Yes." He smiled, revealing his jagged tooth once again.

"What other things do you like to do?"

"Train, train, chooo! Chooooo!" he said, smiling. John enjoys riding the trains and watching them pass by at the station. He waves his hand as they go, calling after them, "Bye bye!"

"Do you like to walk in the park, listen to the birds sing and watch the puppies with their owners?"

"Yes! Yes! Puppies! Puppies! Birds! Birds!"

"Do you like going to the zoo to see the animals?"

"Yes! Yes!" he said, picking up an animal magazine from the desk. He pointed to a photo with a penguin on it and gave it a kiss.

"Would you like to participate in the sports games again like you did last year, John?" I showed him a picture of the team from the previous year, which was pinned to the office wall.

"Yes! Yes!" he said, smiling at the photo.

"You had a great time in the games, didn't you? Hitting the target with the balls, throwing the javelin, dancing and running in the relay with Gemma."

"Yes! Yes! Games! Games! Ball! Ball!" He gestured with his hands as if he were throwing a ball.

"You really enjoyed throwing balls into the basket!" I said, remembering John throwing balls as quickly as he could and not stopping once the game was over. He was laughing out loud, very excited when he managed to sneak one into the basket after the game had ended.

"Tell me something you don't like."

"Noise! Noise!" he said, covering his ears with his hands. "No! No!" He shook his head.

Unfortunately, the length of the conversation began to distract John at this point. He finds it difficult to engage for long periods of time when talking, and he began to yawn.

"Are you tired, John?"

"Yes. Yeaaaahhh," he replied. His last words were taken over by a big yawn.

Before John went to his room, he showed me the drawing he had done of some balls and a basket. "Games! Games!" he said, pointing at the picture. He pinned it near the photo of the Star Team on the office board and went to his room, blowing me a kiss. "Na night!"

"Sweet dreams!" I replied.

Anne

Anne is a good-looking lady with more Latin features than English. She has medium brown hair and eyes and is slim and always impeccably dressed. Despite her slight learning disability and autism, Anne communicates using short but well-coordinated phrases and has excellent manners. She enjoys going out and about with support workers, and during her hours of support, we normally accompany her to her favourite leisure activities. She finds it difficult to handle money, so her helpers give her a hand to double check her transactions and be sure she gives people the correct amount when paying. This helps her to avoid any financial mistakes and also helps to protect her against those who might take advantage of her situation.

After watching *Johnny English* at the cinema – which Anne certainly enjoyed, judging by how she was doubled up with laughter for most of the movie – we sat in the cafeteria at the cinema complex and drank a cappuccino while reliving some of the funny moments from the movie.

"Anne, the day of the sports games is approaching. Are you going to participate this year?" I asked once the movie chatter had died away.

"Oh! Yes, of course. Last year I won the silver medal in the speed race, and this year I would like to be the first," she said proudly with a big smile on her face.

"It sounds like you are really looking forward to it."

"Yes. We had a great time the last couple of years we participated, even though we didn't make it to the finals yet. It really doesn't matter because the important thing is to participate and have fun all together, right, Elisa?"

"Of course. It is an event to compete at, but above all, the idea is to have fun with your mates. Something to look forward to every year." Anne nodded in agreement.

"Anne, besides being a champion, you are also a very active person, and I would like you to tell me a bit about yourself. Family, friends, and hobbies and suchlike. Maybe a little about your life leading up to today, if you don't mind."

"I don't mind telling some things about myself, Elisa. Well, where can I start?" she said, smiling. "I am thirty-seven years old, and as you know, I am half English, half Italian." She paused, took a deep breath and continued. "My father is English and my mother is Sicilian. Farlo italiano un po." She spoke with a very good Italian accent and gestured with her right hand in a typical Italian manner.

"Do you have any brothers or sisters?" I asked.

"I have an older sister. Claudia is married to Sam, and they have two children, a boy and a girl."

"Are you still living with your parents?"

"I still live with my parents, and I like being with them because I am a family-orientated person. I have aunts and uncles, and I also have my two maternal grandparents that I visit often."

"Do you usually go on vacation with your family?"

"Almost every summer, we go to my mother's town in Sicily for two weeks. There I have my cousins and my mother's family, with whom I practise Italian."

"How was your childhood?"

"My childhood was good. All day playing and getting up to mischief with my sister!" she said, laughing.

"Who is your best friend?"

"My friend Sheryl. We used to go to the same special school when we were little. I am still in contact with her. We meet some Saturdays to go to the movies and then have coffee and catch up."

"Apart from Sheryl, do you have any other friends?"

"Yes. I have friends from the day centre where I go on Mondays, and Arthur, whom I meet almost every Saturday at Morrisons cafeteria to have lunch and chat."

"Surely he tells you all the movies he has seen lately in the cinema," I joked. Anne started to laugh.

"Yes. Arthur always talks about movies or the gossip from Star House."

"What kind of movies do you like?"

"I like comedies like the one we have seen today, thrillers, love films, but I hate terror films. They make my hair stand on end!" she said, making a face of disgust and moving her head from side to side in a sign of denial. "Do you like scary movies?" she asked.

"Oh no! I don't like them at all. They make me very nervous. I prefer comedies or movies based on real events," I replied. "What other hobbies do you have apart from going to the cinema?"

"I have a lot of hobbies. I like pantomimes at the theatre, dancing, cooking delicious cakes, singing at the karaoke. What are your hobbies, Elisa?"

"I also like some similar things; I like going to the movies, theatre and dance. Though I don't know how to cook or sing! I like to read historical or adventure novels, but overall, I am most passionate about travelling, and every time I can, I escape to a different place. Tell me a little about your activities during the week," I asked.

"On Mondays I go to a day centre from nine in the morning to four in the afternoon."

"What activities do you do at the day centre?"

"We do different activities. Some days we cook our own food, other days we make art and crafts, and when the weather is good, we do excursions around the town. On Tuesdays I go to a rock choir. Wednesdays I have a few hours of support to do things that I like. Sometimes we do group activities with Arthur, Matthew and Eric."

"What activities have you done recently with them? What do you enjoy doing the most?"

"I enjoyed the excursion to Francis Bacon's house last summer. It was a great day! We saw sheep, cows and horses grazing in the meadows. Last Christmas we went to the Winter Wonderland at Hyde Park in London. Two weeks ago we went to the Sky Garden, where we had great views of Tower Bridge and the Tower of London. A few weeks before that, we went to the Tate Modern and last week to the Natural History Museum. I really like London. Do you like London?"

"I love London, Anne! I fell in love immediately the first time I visited it many years ago. All the people from different countries and cultures, its amazing architecture, and all the fascinating monuments everywhere. Big Ben, the Tower of London and Buckingham Palace. Double-decker buses and black taxis and red mailboxes. Museums, markets, pubs, nightlife and so many activities to enjoy twenty-four hours a day. I never get tired of London! As Dr Samuel Johnson said, 'When a man is tired of London, he is tired of life.' Oh, Anne, I really love London. I could talk about it for hours!"

"We are very lucky, aren't we, Elisa? We live so close, we can go whenever we like."

"Absolutely! The next group activity I am planning for you, Andrew, Matthew and Eric will be to watch a Shakespeare play at the Globe this summer, as I know all of you love plays."

"That will be great! I've never been to the Globe or watched a Shakespeare play." Anne smiled enthusiastically at the plan.

"So, Anne, I understand you do some volunteering work?"

"Yes. On Thursdays I volunteer. Four hours in an Oxfam charity shop, and on Fridays in a coffee shop making cakes."

"And the weekends?"

"On Saturdays I sometimes meet my friend Sheryl and sometimes I meet with Arthur for lunch at Morrisons. I always spend Sundays with my family, as my sister and her family normally come to have lunch at home."

"You are a woman with a busy agenda!"

She laughed. "Yes. I am a busy lady!"

"What kinds of thing don't you like?"

"Greys. Dark and rainy days depress me. Uhmm, horror movies and funerals and being away from home for a long time."

"Have you had any sad experiences in the past that made you unhappy?"

"Yes. A few years ago, my auntie Lucy passed away from a sudden illness. We were very close. I loved her so much and I felt very upset. For a long time, I couldn't eat or sleep well because I missed her. I still miss her a lot." Anne had tears in her eyes as she remembered.

"It's normal to feel depressed when you lose someone you love. I also experienced a particularly sad episode in my childhood. When I was thirteen, I had to deal with the unexpected death of one of my best friends at school. I can still remember her laughing, because she laughed at everything, and her laughter was so infectious. That was the second time that I had to face the loss of a loved one, and it left me depressed for a long time."

"I am so sorry, Elisa. I didn't know."

"Don't worry. This is part of life. The best we can do is try to accept it and not let the memories of people we loved die in our hearts. We have to carry on with our life and make as much as we can of it. Let's change the subject. Tell me, what are your plans for the future?"

"I would like to find a job where I get paid. Amanda, my key worker, is helping me prepare my CV to look for work in coffee shops where I can work as a kitchen assistant or prepare cakes, which is what I do best."

"Would you like to live independently in your own apartment in the future?"

"Yes, I would like to live in my own apartment one day, but I am not in a hurry, because with my parents I am very happy."

"Thank you, Anne, for telling me things about yourself. It will be very useful – a great help for me, to be sure. I will organise activities that you like."

"The pleasure has been mine, Elisa," she replied politely.

Once Anne had finished her cappuccino, I accompanied her as we travelled to her home by bus. "Ciao bella," I called as she stepped off the bus.

"Grazie mille ragazza!" She waved with a smile.

Eric

Eric is a 67-year-old gentleman with mild autism. Last week I accompanied him to a general check-up with his GP at the local health centre near the small apartment where he lives independently. While we were waiting in the surgery reception, Eric started calling out to the receptionist.

"Excuse me, sir! Excuse me, sir!" he called out loudly, almost shouting.

"Eric, that's not a man, it's a lady!" I said when I realised. As the receptionist approached the counter, Eric frowned.

"Oh! I'm sorry if I called you sir, but you look like a man." Eric spoke quite innocently, but I felt embarrassed as the words hung in the air. My cheeks burned, though in truth I thought the same as he did. The lady had very masculine features and dark whiskers atop her upper lip. I felt uncomfortable but somewhat in admiration of Eric's direct sincerity.

"Eric, would you mind going to the waiting room while I give your details to the receptionist?" I asked him to avoid any further embarrassment.

After his annual health check-up – all the results were good except for slightly high cholesterol, which Eric already controls with medication – we went to complete his weekly food shop with the list that we had prepared beforehand. "Are we going to do your shopping at the Spar or shall we go to Morrisons?" I gave him a choice.

"What? Excuse me, Elisa, could you say that again? I didn't hear you." He spoke loudly, holding his hands to his ears. I realised that once again he was not wearing his hearing aids.

"Eric, you don't hear me because you don't wear the gadgets," I scolded him. He pulled a box from his pocket, where he was carrying his hearing aids, and placed them one by one into his ears.

"Now I can hear you. I don't wear them all the time to save battery," he said, this time without yelling.

"Well, you have to wear them all the time, Eric. When the battery runs out, you can go to the hospital and they will give you new ones for free." He nodded while undoubtedly thinking about doing whatever he wanted once he was alone again. "Shall we go to the Spar or Morrisons for your shopping?" I asked him again.

"We'd better go to the Spar that is close to home, because Morrisons is far away to get back loaded with all the shopping," he said thoughtfully.

"Great! The Spar it is, then."

"Okay, Elisa. But let's be careful. I don't want to overspend my shopping money for the week!"

"Of course. Don't worry. We won't spend too much."

Eric was forever careful to remind us whenever it was time to spend money. It was always very important not to spend too much! We headed off to walk to the Spar nearby.

"How was your week, Eric?"

While rolling a cigarette, he explained what he had been up to during the week. "The weekend was relaxed. I spent most of the time watching Western films and listening to country music. On Monday I met Susan for lunch, and afterwards we went to the supermarket to buy some bits for Susan, then I accompanied Susan back to her residential home. Yesterday I went to the bank with Alex to take out the money for this week, because today I couldn't go, as I had my annual check-up."

We arrived at the Spar, and once the purchases had been made, we headed back to his apartment. Once we arrived, we tidied up everything in the cupboards and fridge and packed away the shopping. We sat down to rest for a while in the living room with a cup of tea. We listened to a radio channel on the television that was playing his favourite country music. I noticed a new photo on the window ledge, so I walked over to take a look. The picture was recent. It was Eric with his six brothers and sisters, all of them older. Eric, with his white hair, stood next to his two bald brothers. Everyone was somewhat overweight except for Eric, who is the most athletic of the family. His white hair looks like it has been stuck on between his ears, and he has a Chuck Norris–style moustache. He was smiling for the photo, showing the gaps in his teeth, and he was wearing a blue plaid shirt tucked into his chinos.

"It's me and my brothers. We are five brothers and two sisters. We took this picture two years ago at Christmas, and one of my

76

sisters recently sent it to me as a souvenir, as Paul and Alfred died recently." He pointed out the two deceased brothers.

"I'm so sorry, Eric. I didn't know," I said, surprised. I hadn't seen him for some time.

"Do you have family, Elisa?"

"Yes. My parents, my two brothers, a nephew and two nieces, along with the rest of the family. They all live in Spain," I replied.

Eric sighed. "You are lucky that everyone is alive. We are also lucky to still be around, aren't we, Elisa?"

"Well, we have to enjoy the moment, because we don't know when we are going to leave. If you feel like it, you can tell me about your childhood and your family." I encouraged him to talk, as I noticed he was quite sad over the recent death of his brothers.

"When I was little, I used to live with my parents and my brothers. I used to play with all my siblings, but especially with the younger ones, as we were closer in age. I don't really remember much of my childhood because when I was eight years old, my parents sent me to a special boarding school, and afterwards I went to live in the hospital from 1962 to 1977. After that, I lived in several shared houses until I moved into this flat, where I have lived on my own since 1995." He made this short summary of his life with few sentences and with exact dates because he is very good at remembering dates and years.

"Do you like living independently?"

"Oh! Yes, Elisa. I can do what I want."

"What memories do you have of living in the hospital?"

"There I met Hector, Catherine, Jim and many others. It wasn't bad, but I prefer to live in my own apartment and have the freedom to do what I want. I like preparing my own food, getting up and going to bed when I feel like it, listening to music or playing music on my piano without disturbing anyone."

"What kinds of music do you like?"

"I like different styles of music and groups, such as The Beatles, Gilbert O'Sullivan, Abba, The Searchers, The Shadows, all the music of the fifties, sixties, seventies and eighties and some songs of the nineties," he said, pointing to and approaching a huge pile of CDs, records and old tapes stacked in a corner of the room.

"You have a big collection of music, Eric! How do you manage to listen to the old tapes and records?" I was surprised, as nowadays these formats are not in use.

"I have a new tablet where I can hear as much music as I like, but I enjoy playing my old tapes and records every now and then." He took an old record player and a cassette deck from the closet.

"Do these artefacts even still work?" I asked with some humour, as the cassette deck looked like it belonged to the age of the dinosaurs.

"Oh yes! Look, I'm going to play a Gilbert O'Sullivan tape so you can see how it works." He put the cassette into the player and pressed hard on the chunky Play button. What came out sounded mostly like Gilbert O'Sullivan, though it was obviously a very old tape.

"Oh! It does work, although it sounds a bit fuzzy. Maybe it needs a good clean or perhaps you need a new one. Is that the tape that Gilbert O'Sullivan autographed when we went to one of his concerts?"

"Yes! It was a wonderful concert. Do you remember we went together? Look at the autograph!" He handed me the cassette box and I could see the autograph and the dedication of Gilbert O'Sullivan. I smiled as I was reminded of the surprised face of Gilbert when Eric had passed him the thirty-year-old tape to be autographed.

"You know how to play the piano, you say?" I pointed to an old electronic organ that was standing next to the huge stack of tapes, records and CDs. By the look of it, it must have been more or less the same age as the cassette deck or the record player, maybe even older.

"Yes, I do. I know how to play some songs. I'm going to play one so you can see how smart I am." He became very excited as he approached the old organ. He played "Happy Birthday" and then "Daisy, Daisy".

"Apart from playing the organ, what other hobbies do you have?"

"I have a lot of hobbies. On Thursdays I normally go to play pool with a group during my support hours. On Friday mornings I go to an art and painting course where I see my girlfriend Susan. I also like to go to music concerts, comedies, theatres, movies." He paused to take a deep breath and continued. "I like to go to the birthdays of my friends and all the parties and barbecues they invite me to at Star House."

He became more animated and happy as he went on. "Do you know that I celebrated my sixty-seventh birthday at the Crown pub, where we met many friends, and I took the chance at the party to give Susan an engagement ring that I bought in Argos very cheap? It was a very fun party!"

Susan is a few years older than Eric, and although she has mental and other health problems, she remains an active person. She is of medium height and somewhat plump, with a toothless smile. Her hair is white, and she usually wears it in a mid-length bob, which, along with her colourful dresses, white socks and cream shoes, gives her a youthful look. "Isn't she wonderful?" Eric says every time he sees her, admiring her as proudly as if she were Audrey Hepburn.

"How long have you been dating Susan?"

"I've been dating her for three years now. Susan is my first formal girlfriend – in fact the only girlfriend I've ever had. You know that, Elisa? I met her at the arts and crafts course that we both attend on Fridays. We connected very well with each other from the beginning and fell in love. Since then, we meet almost every day, and we enjoy having lunch together, going to the cinema, walking and shopping." Eric paused to take a drink.

"Last year we went on holiday to Great Yarmouth, a beautiful seaside town where we had a great week together! Look what Susan gave me when we were there." He fetched a teddy bear with a big red heart that he had on the living room window ledge next to the photo of him and his siblings. He started hugging and kissing the bear tenderly. "Isn't he so wonderful, Elisa? I'm a soft-hearted man!" He carried on kissing the teddy.

"Are you going on holiday again this year?"

"We would like to go to Blackpool this year," he said excitedly, kissing the stuffed teddy some more.

"Tell me about your work life." I changed the subject.

"I have had different jobs in the past. When I lived in the hospital, I was a kitchen assistant. Then I worked for a while in a clothing store in the shopping centre as a cleaning assistant and finally in a French restaurant as a kitchen assistant for more than twenty years until I retired two years ago."

"Wow! You've worked hard in your life." I praised him.

"Yes. That's why today I have my pension and I can spend my time doing the things I like," he said proudly.

"Ah! What about sports? Are you and Susan thinking of participating in the games this year?" I asked, as I noticed a bronze medal hung on the kitchen wall.

"Yes! Last year we had a great time at the sports games. We won some of the events and I finished third in the relay race." He took the bronze medal down from the wall and handed it to me. "But overall we didn't manage to be finalists, you know. Let's see if we have more luck this year and win a prise!" He laughed, rubbing his hands enthusiastically.

"Apart from participating in the games, what are your expectations for the near future?"

"I would like to move to a bigger apartment with Susan. Our social workers are studying our case, but the paperwork is taking ages. With our age and Susan's health, I don't know if I will be left without a girlfriend before we can manage to live together. Anyway" – he sighed – "we'll see what happens."

"After all this talk, you must be hungry. What do you fancy for dinner?" I had to suggest dinner otherwise he would have chattered on for ages and forgotten all about food.

"I feel like some sausages with mashed potatoes and vegetables," he said as he began to take out the ingredients from the fridge.

"I can help you out if you want."

"Oh no. I can do it alone without help. I am a grown-up man. Thanks for the conversation and for the time, but I don't need anything else. When I have prepared dinner, I would like to sit down to eat quietly while I watch my favourite programme, *Who Wants to Be a Millionaire*," he said, pointing to the exit, and with that I understood that it was time for me to leave.

"Until next week!" I said, closing the door behind me before he closed it on my nose!

Charlotte

A few days before Christmas, I met Charlotte in a quiet local pub for a drink and a chat about her recent appearance on a television programme where people are put in contact with each other to go on a date.

"Hi, Charlotte. Thanks for meeting with me. I can't wait to hear about your love story and your experience on *television*! But first of all, I would like you to tell me where your last name comes from. A colleague from work has mentioned it, and I want you to confirm the story."

"Ah! Yes. My grandfather was president of an African country." She said this as if to have a grandfather who was the president of another country were the most natural thing in the world!

"I thought you were popular because of your appearance on *the show*, which is well-known in England, but now I discover that you are also a president's granddaughter! This is going to be a very interesting interview."

"My experience being on *television* has changed my life. I couldn't have imagined when you suggested I look for a partner through the show that it would lead to where I am today. I was very excited with the idea from the first moment you mentioned it, but I never thought it would all happen so quickly. Days after making the application online, the programme called me to do an interview via Skype where I introduced myself and gave them the profile of the person I was looking for. A week later, they called me again to say they had a candidate matching the profile I had given them. They asked if I would like to be filmed for the programme, and I accepted. It happened so fast that I haven't had time for it all to sink in yet!" she said excitedly.

"It was a surprise for me too. I suggested that you contact *organisers of the dating programme* because I knew you were looking for a partner, and I like watching the programme so much myself, I thought it would be a great idea for you to take part in it. When Christopher, your key worker, who sent your application, called me to let me know that the programme had contacted you, I couldn't believe it!"

"I couldn't believe it either. It still seems like a dream," said Charlotte, holding her hands to her cheeks.

"So, my very first recording for the show, I was introduced to Stephen. It was love at first sight! I liked him from the beginning. He is a good person. A gentleman with a good sense of humour. To be honest, Elisa, I couldn't have asked for more!" Charlotte took a sip of her tea and continued with the story. "Meeting Stephen has given me confidence in myself, because in the past, I have had bad experiences in romantic relationships. I always ended up feeling insecure and with low self-esteem. I had lost hope of finding someone special in my life. Then Stephen appeared that day and was all I was looking for in a partner. He has given me back happiness and the belief in love."

"That's great! It isn't easy to find a person with whom you connect in every way. I also haven't lost hope of one day finding someone special," I said sincerely.

"We connected from the first moment we met. We kept in touch, and since then, we have created a strong relationship. I can't explain in words what Stephen means to me. The relationship becomes stronger and more serious every day. After our vacation which was recorded by the programme's producers, we decided to introduce our families to each other to formalise our relationship."

"I can see how happy you are."

"I'm very happy. Thank you very much for giving me the idea of participating in the programme and finding Stephen. We are very happy together, and now I have the motivation to get up every day."

"How is fame affecting you? Do people stop you on the street?"

"Oh my gosh! I love the popularity. People have stopped me on the street to ask if it's me who appeared *on television* and I feel like a celebrity!" Charlotte laughed.

"I'm very happy that things are going so well for you now. Would you like to tell me a few more things about your life, your childhood and your family so I can get to know a little more about you?"

"Yes, of course. Where can I start? Umm ..." She stopped to think for a few seconds. "I spent many years at a Catholic boarding school for girls until I was eighteen years old. There I made many friends, and I still keep in touch with some of them. I used to be a sporty girl. I did drama classes, and I used to do horse riding and did work on a farm taking care of animals. I remember when I turned eighteen. My mother organised a party at the school that turned out to be the most boring birthday I'd ever had, because the nuns were very strict and didn't allow boys, alcoholic drinks or any of the mischief typical of an eighteen-year-old! We ended up dancing to religious songs with the nuns. A whole lot of boredom!" She started laughing, remembering her own story, and I found myself laughing along too.

"What about your parents? Do you have siblings?"

"My parents met at the hospital where they worked. My father was a doctor and my mother an Irish nurse. They fell in love and here I am – a 48-year-old mulatto with afro curly black hair, nice and somewhat meaty but really good-looking!" She gestured up and down the length of her body, giggling. "Then my three brothers were born after me. Years later, my parents divorced and followed their own paths." She paused. "As well as my three brothers, I have two stepsisters and a stepbrother from my father's second marriage."

"Which of them are you close with?"

"I get along with everyone in general, but the one I am closest to is my brother Anthony, who lives in the same town. We see each other often."

"Do you have contact with your parents?"

"I see my mother quite a lot. We are very close, although sometimes we have our differences and we quarrel. I don't have as much contact with my father, as he lives far away. We used to call each other often, but since he was diagnosed with Alzheimer's disease, we hardly speak now, because I feel sorry that he doesn't recognise me. I want to go see him sometime soon anyway." She sighed with a little sadness.

"How were your teen years?"

"Ha! Elisa! I was a diva. Whenever I could, I loved dancing at the discos and flirting with the boys, but unfortunately I started to have problems with my mental health around age fifteen. I began to suffer from self-destructive behaviours and self-harming. I attempted suicide twice. I was diagnosed with bipolar depression." With this, her tone changed dramatically as she held back tears. "Since then I have spent my life going from therapy to therapy. Psychologists, psychiatrists, hospitals and medication. My treatment helps me to have a mental balance, though it is not easy, and sometimes in stressful situations I lose control of my actions."

"How do you handle your mental illness?"

"My mental problem is very difficult to control," she said with her eyes down. "It's like a roller coaster. Up! Down! During my low moments, I feel dizziness and a horrible depression where nothing makes sense. I have to work very hard every day to avoid falling down the well of self-destruction."

"What therapies help you with your mental balance?"

"Apart from medical treatment, I try other natural therapies such as art that help me to express myself by getting out bad thoughts and feelings. Walking in the park relaxes me. I like to go for walks with my support worker and chat about things. I also go swimming. In general, sporting activities help me. I recently started a diary where each day I write and draw my feelings. I always carry it here in my bag."

She took out her diary and handed it over. I flipped through some of the pages to see what she had written and drawn. Some days she showed how bad she felt, representing her emotions with drawings of black skulls, blood and daggers. Other days she wrote positively and drew pictures of hearts and smiles with rainbows of bright colours.

"Do you receive any emotional support from your family and friends?"

"Yes. I have support from my family, psychologists and the organisation that provides me with hours of support, but the greatest and most important support in my life come from my best friend, Nora." Nora lives in the same building as Charlotte and also has mental health difficulties in addition to a serious eating disorder.

"She is the most important person in my life. She is my rock. She is always there for me through my good and bad times. Nora loves me the way I am, and we laugh together at our problems." Tears showed again in Charlotte's eyes as she spoke of Nora.

"That is a beautiful friendship, Charlotte. You are lucky to have each other." I had tears of my own welling up as I listened to her.

"Yes. I'm very lucky to have a friend like Nora. She makes me laugh a lot with her good sense of humour."

"I have seen you both on more than one occasion telling naughty jokes in the communal lounge of the building. I still remember the joke about Superman!"

"Oh yes! Why does Superman wear his suit under his underpants? So he doesn't leave a mark on his pants!" We both laughed. "Yes, we can't help ourselves with naughty jokes. They are our weakness," she said, still laughing.

"Does Nora know Stephen?"

"Yes, and they connect very well. Nora's approval is very important to me, so I'm very happy that they get along so well."

"Tell me what your life is like living independently at Albion Supported Living."

"I've been living independently in my current apartment for seventeen years now. I can't believe how quickly the time has passed! When I left boarding school, I went to live in a sheltered house shared with other girls with mental health issues for many years. Social services offered me one of the nine apartments at Albion Supporting Living, where other people with learning disabilities or mental problems live. The building has 24-hour assistance in case we need any help, in addition to having individual support hours with support workers to help with leisure activities. We also have a communal lounge where neighbours get together to socialise, drink tea and listen to music. We can watch television together too, have our meals and arrange parties. There I have spent some very good times with my neighbours."

"Do you get along with all of your neighbours?"

"In general, I get along with everyone, but I'm most attached to Rachel, Hazel and of course my best friend Nora."

"Ah! Before I forget, I would like to ask you if you are going to participate next year in the Hertfordshire sports games with your friends from the building as the Moon Team?"

"Sure, Elisa. I'm looking forward to it. I'm keeping up my physical fitness with swimming and walking. We had a great time at the event. It is a group activity that we all enjoy together that lets us leave aside our differences and focus on the competition. I hope this year we get first place, since we are all very well-prepared and eager to give it everything we can," she said, smiling and very confident.

"Yes, the truth is that you have a good team. Most of you are in good physical shape. Well, Charlotte, apart from the games, let me ask one last question. What are your plans for the future?"

"Well, for now I will continue to see Stephen and we will record some more episodes of *the show*. The next recording will be for Christmas, when we are going to join my family and Stephen's family at my brother's house."

With that, it was time to go. As we left the pub, Charlotte began to sing "All I want for Christmas is Stephen!" She was laughing loudly.

The Games

I woke up to a morning of 24-degree sunshine – a perfect day of English weather and a bright start to the day of the games!

We had agreed that everyone would meet at Star House at nine a.m. This would leave plenty of time for Amanda to drive the clunky rented minibus to the venue. Sure enough, as I rounded the final corner of my walk to work, I could see people ready and waiting. Anne, Matthew, Catherine, Eric and Susan had all arrived in good time and were standing outside chatting, while Arthur, Ron, John and Hector were waiting indoors. I could see Arthur by the window, anxiously peering through the curtains looking for any sign of the minibus.

Everyone was all geared up for the day, dressed in all manner of shorts, T-shirts, leggings and running shoes. Almost everyone, I should say. Eric had decided that he was going to attend in his own unique Chuck Norris style – a light blue formal shirt and dark blue chinos with Aviator sunglasses and a smart pair of black shoes. With Eric was his girlfriend Susan, and, not to be outdone, Susan was also dressed very smartly in her favourite colourful fuchsia print dress with patterned socks and cream shoes. Perhaps not the best clothes for a sports day, but they were both happy and full of enthusiasm for the day to come.

"The bus has arrived!" Arthur alerted everyone from his post at the window.

"Let's go! Let's go!" shouted Hector.

For a moment, nobody paid much attention. Arthur had proclaimed the bus's arrival on sighting at least three different cars and a bin lorry, and Hector had been telling everyone to "Let's go! Let's go!" every ten minutes for the past hour. But then, sure enough, we all heard the noise of the bus and the squeak of the brakes as it pulled up to the front of Star House. The level of excitement jumped up a notch as everyone began collecting bags, helping with equipment and generally fussing about while all trying to get into the bus at the same time.

"Let's go! Let's go!" Hector called again as Alex pushed his wheelchair towards the minibus.

"Hector! Don't yell!" Catherine yelled at him, shushing him just for a moment.

There was a flurry of busy-work as the support workers organised everyone one by one into the bus and stacked all the backpacks and equipment around and underneath the seats. The packed lunches, the gazebo, lots of sunscreen, spare clothes, plenty of bottled water and various other bits and pieces were all somehow squeezed into the back of the minibus.

We made it to the sports facilities just in time, and once the minibus was parked, the excited group of participants disembarked and took all of the equipment we had with us. We needed to get registered as competitors, find our spot, set up the gazebo and make the Star Team camp. We could see a large open area edged with trees that was split into two different spaces. One side was marked out for playing the various games, and the other was set up for the teams to make their home spaces and picnic areas. As we began to walk over, we were met by some of the organisers and volunteers holding clipboards and carrying a box of T-shirts.

"Are you the Star Team?" they called. "Let's get the names checked and your T-shirts handed out. You guys are the last ones to arrive!"

I spoke with the organisers and checked we had all the names expected on the list. Once that was done, competitors and support staff alike were handed yellow T-shirts with "Star Team" printed across the front. Ron was especially pleased with his T-shirt. "We are going to win this year!" he proclaimed, cheering loudly and waving his T-shirt like a flag.

"Yes! We are going to win!"

"Winners! Winners!" Everyone cheered and laughed.

We made our way over to the team home area. We could see that the other teams were busy getting themselves set up and organised. It all looked very colourful in the sunshine, with each team wearing their own brightly coloured shirts. Alex and Tendai set up our gazebo, while Arthur and Ron were very interested in sorting out and arranging the packed lunches and other food, no doubt with the intention of sneaking a snack into their pockets when nobody was looking.

It didn't take long for friends from other teams to notice we had arrived and come over to say hello.

"Hello, Marc!" John greeted his friend with an energetic hug.

"Nice to see you around, John. I will see you later for a drink and chit-chat. Bye!" Marc greeted John, abruptly said goodbye with a wave and walked back to his teammates.

"Bye bye, Marc." John waved back at him.

It made me smile to watch their short but sweet hello and goodbye. There was an innocence that shone through as Marc and John greeted each other. After all, these two were great friends, and you would normally expect such good friends to chatter on a little when saying hello. Instead, though, a simple "hello" and "goodbye" was all they needed to bring smiles to their faces and settle them into the occasion, knowing their best friend was close by.

Ron's day became a little bit sunnier as he caught the eye of his girlfriend, Agnes. She had arrived on a different minibus, as she was participating with a different team. They both bounced up and down a little, flashing a smile and a big wave across to each other.

"See you at break time, honey!" she shouted over, bringing a little colour to Ron's cheeks.

"Attention, teams!" The megaphone crackled loudly as the organisers made the first announcement of the day. "The first games will begin in fifteen minutes!"

With the starting announcement, everyone headed back to their own team camp, and while everything seemed to quieten down a little, within each team the excitement crept higher.

I read over the guide that had been handed out by the organisers to get an idea of how the day was to go. There were a number of different activity areas set out around the field. These were for games like javelin or basketball, where the participating members of each team would take several turns to achieve the best score they could for each activity. There would be around fifteen minutes spent on each task and then the teams would rotate around to the next area. Once the initial set of games had been played through by all the teams, there would be a short break for lunch. After lunch, the teams would then nominate the competitors for participation in the afternoon's races.

The megaphone boomed out once more. "Could all teams please approach their game areas."

Star Team headed over as a group to the game area that was marked out for them and waited for the call to begin. The first game was the javelin throw. The javelins were made of plastic with rubber tips, because real javelins can be dangerous even when you've been trained to throw one. Each team member was to take a few turns at throwing the javelin as far as possible, and their best throw would contribute to the team's score. The Star Team members took their turns, and everything was going smoothly until John made his last throw.

"Oh *no!*" I heard gasps from some of the other Star Team members. I turned around to see John with a worried look on his face and a javelin several feet away in the opposite direction to the one intended, stuck into the ground next to a smiling but flustered event judge!

After the javelin incident, the next few games were thankfully uneventful. Star Team was doing quite well, although we hadn't quite managed to keep up with the leaders. Lunchtime was getting closer, and Arthur and Ron were both predictably beginning to get somewhat distracted at the thought of sandwiches and cakes. However, before they could sit down to eat, there was one more event to go, and it promised to work up everyone's appetite.

It was time for some dancing! The dancing event turned out to be the funniest of all. Everyone on the team, including the staff, had a very entertaining time as we all tried to keep up with the instructor and in time with the music. "Arms up! Arms down! Move your hips and turn around!" the instructor called out and moved in time to the music, accompanied by a mostly coordinated if occasionally freestyle response from the Star Team competitors. Right away, it was apparent that Anne was the dance expert. She even recognised the song they were dancing to and was singing along with all her heart, arms up and arms down and spinning around just as the instructor was calling out.

The story was a little different across the other members of the team, however. Ron, Eric and Matthew were doing their best, but the coordination required to listen to the beat of the music and follow along with the moves proved a bit too much. A variety of mixed-up moves and out-of-time spinning was the best they could manage. They didn't care, though, and judging by their smiles and energetic enthusiasm, they were having great fun! Arthur was in his own world, and, while he was easily keeping time with the music, he had decided, as he always did whenever dancing was involved, that his ski-style dance moves were the order of the day. Hector was determined that being in a wheelchair wasn't going to stop him from joining in, and he was waving, stretching and calling out "Amen!" and the occasional "Lazy lump!" with surprising energy for the oldest member of the team. It seemed a little chaotic, but all things considered, everybody was really doing quite well. Eventually the music came to an end, leaving everybody exhausted, hungry and looking forward to lunchtime.

The morning's events had finished and it was time to take a break and relax for a while – grab something to eat and spend some time recuperating and getting ready for the second half of the day. We had brought along some sandwiches and other tasty treats, and we spent some time setting out a picnic under our gazebo in the shade of a large tree. As we sat down for lunch, Ron's girlfriend, Agnes, came over to say hello and steal a sandwich from his plate.

"Hey!" he called out and was about to take it back when she leaned in to put her arm around his shoulders and plant a kiss on his cheek. He quickly forgot about his missing sandwich. "Did you see me scoring at basketball?" he asked her. "I scored most of the baskets for the team!" He puffed up his chest with pride.

"Oooh, well done!" Agnes replied and gave him a big hug.

Hector, Catherine, Anne and Matthew had found themselves a nice sunny patch of grass and were sitting cross-legged, chatting. Matthew must have been talking about his prowess with the bow and arrow, as he was acting out holding up the bow and loosing an arrow.

"Who wants a cup of tea?" Ron was offering to make a round of tea for everyone.

"Yes, please!" Agnes replied.

I called out, "Two sugars, but only a little spot of milk, please."

"Me too!" said Anne.

I helped Ron to make the tea and made sure he had the right amounts of sugar and tea for everyone. If we weren't careful, he would quite happily give everyone four teabags and five sugars! Once they were brewed, Ron handed Agnes and Anne their cups of tea and sat down quietly next to Agnes to focus on eating his sandwiches.

Arthur was in chatterbox mode and was talking to anyone that would listen. "Did you see when John threw the javelin? He nearly hit the lady! I really enjoyed the archery contest. I hadn't fired a bow for a long time! How are the other teams doing? Do we know our scores at the moment?"

John was sitting quietly in the shade of a nearby tree, eating his lunch and listening to the hubbub of people and the tweeting of the birds in the trees. The support workers, Kelly and Alex, were sitting next to John and chattering quietly together. It only took a moment to see there was chemistry between them. The telltale signs of young love were written in Alex's unwavering gaze and Kelly's affectionate touch – the sing-song notes as they laughed together as they remembered the morning's events.

Charlotte from the Moon Team came wandering over with her best friend, Nora. You had to be careful with these two; there could be a certain crude edge to their humour. I had already noticed them using phrases like "tight buns" and giggling as they watched a couple of the male event organisers.

"Hey, Star Team! How is that score coming along?" Charlotte asked.

"We're doing very well, we think, but we won't know our final score until they give the results at the end," Arthur replied, gesturing enthusiastically with his hands as he always does.

"Well, good luck to all of you! My team, Moon Team, is scoring a lot of points. Maybe this year we will be among the finalists again!" Nora said with confidence, smiling broadly.

"Yes, we will be the winners again this year!" said Hazel, a fellow Moon Team member who had also come over to see what was going on.

"It really doesn't matter who wins. We're all having good time, aren't we?" Arthur replied, though the end of his sentence disappeared as he enthusiastically started on one of the cakes that had been provided by the event organisers for lunch. "Would you like one? They're free!" Arthur offered them the cakes.

"Thank you, Arthur, but Nora and I are just passing by. We need to go and collect some of the drinks we brought along for our team before we all fall over from thirst!"

"Oh! Yes, please!" said Hazel. "I've already had one, but I don't mind another. We're burning a lot of calories today, after all." She gladly accepted a cake and sat down beside Arthur.

They carried on talking and giggling while eating and drinking tea until it was time for the organisers to call the teams together once more and ready everyone for the second session of the games.

The second half of the day was for the racing events, where a few members of each team would race against each other. There was to be a sprint, hurdles, a wheelchair race and finally a relay race. Anne, Matthew, Arthur and Eric were Star Team's picks for the running races, with Hector our entry for the wheelchair race.

The wheelchair race was the highlight of the afternoon. Hector was more excited than I had seen him in a long time. Alex was Hector's choice of driver, and he proudly stepped up to take the handles of the wheelchair and line up with the other competitors ready for the race to begin.

"Are you Spanish?" Hector called to the starter standing at the line ready to count them off. "Let's go! Let's go!" he shouted out to everyone in general, and the countdown began.

"Ready!"

"Steady!"

"Go!"

Alex gave Hector's wheelchair a great big shove and they were off as fast as his legs could take them. Hector was rolling back and forth in his seat with one arm thrust forward, almost reminiscent of Superman, and his eyes wide open.

"Lazy lump, let's go! Jesus loves us!" Hector exclaimed as they sped off down the track. "Amen!" he called out as they finished in third place.

Then, finally, we came to the last competition of the day – the relay race. Matthew, Anne, Eric and John had been picked for this event. While John did have difficulty seeing clearly, Gemma was to be at his side guiding him along. But Star Team unfortunately didn't make it into the first three.

After a great day of excitement and fun, the organisers called out over the megaphone one final time to gather everybody to the podium. Now was the time to reveal the positions and the medal winners.

"When does the food and refreshment start?" Ron asked out loud, and a few giggles erupted from the group of waiting athletes.

"Yes! When does the meal start?" Arthur added upon being reminded about food and acted out an exaggerated licking of his lips.

"Shhh!" hissed Agnes. "They're about to tell us the winners."

Eric took a silver medal in the archery, Anne had made silver in the hurdles, and Hector, with Alex as his driver, had won bronze in the wheelchair race. When it came to overall team scores, Star Team didn't quite make it into the medals, coming fourth overall. This was generally considered a great triumph considering the level of preparation of the other teams. Moon Team did indeed come first, just as Charlotte had predicted. Although the Star Team members hadn't quite realised their dream of coming first – and indeed not all of the teams had won medals or had gold medal athletes in their ranks – amongst the staff, it was agreed that everyone really was a winner, because for a few hours we had all forgotten the difficulties and troubles of the daily routine.

Once all the results had been called out, medals awarded and hearty cheers and congratulations given to the winners, it was time to relax with a party, and, as with all good parties, this one kicked off with dancing! All the teams joined together, and the familiar music from the dancing event earlier in the day began. Everyone had the opportunity to mingle and get close to best friends and partners. "Hands up and hands down!" Anne was calling out. At some point, everyone was spinning around. Partners were found; some were jiving and some were swinging about. Generally, the moves of the earlier dance event were forgotten, and everyone did their own thing as we all just had fun. It was a very energetic dancing, singing, smiling, laughing-out-loud gathering of wonderful people.

After the dancing came the drinking and the eating. At last! The best part of the event, according to Arthur and Ron. There was a choice of soft drinks, snacks, sandwiches and some cakes, with everyone sitting down to relax and chat and perhaps starting to feel just a little bit tired.

Eventually, it was time to go home. The teams began to organise their things; the gazebos and chairs and picnic paraphernalia and cushions and blankets and all the other accoutrements of the day were slowly collected up and loaded into various minibuses and cars, and, one by one, each began to make their way home. Overall, there was a warm feeling of satisfaction at a lovely day spent amongst wonderful friends.

"Last year we were in fifth and this year in fourth position. We are on the right path, mates. Surely next year we will be in third place!" Eric proclaimed on the minibus on the way home. He was still full of optimism and energy as he held onto his silver medal with one hand while his other arm was around Susan, who was almost asleep beside him. Arthur was sitting quietly, lost in a heart-shaped bubble.

After Eric's proclamation, Arthur gave a sigh of satisfaction and smiled as he said, "Today I didn't win any medals, but Hazel did give me her phone number so we can arrange to meet sometime!"

And with that, the bus fell quiet. A little too quiet, it seemed, but taking a look back to make sure everyone was okay, all I could see was a collection of nodding sleepyheads. It really had been an exhausting day!

It had been a long day for everyone, full of anticipation and energy at a sporting event where everyone shared the values of companionship, respect and discipline. But most important of all was the lesson learned. Winning medals and being the best was not the prize. The prize was spending the day with real friends, forgetting the difficulties of life and living a day filled to the brim with excitement, smiles and laughter.

No matter how high the mountain,
there is always a way to the top.

Afterword

During my half-hour journey to work, I try to connect with the moment, watching, as if at the movies, the people who get on and off the bus. The two old women with white hair, dressed in bright colours, whispering and laughing with each other. The old Chinese man who doesn't speak a word of English but smiles at me and nods his good morning. The middle-aged Sikh gentleman with a long beard, wearing a white robe and with a turban on his head, who looks through the window until he reaches his destination. The black woman and her red-haired husband with twin babies in a double pushchair. The middle-sized lady wearing tie-dyed clothes, with her old greyhound dog that she often takes to the veterinarian in town for a check-up. The group of teenagers wearing school uniform who cannot take their eyes from their mobile phones to talk to each other. The young executive dressed in a jacket and suit, looking constantly and impatiently at his watch until he arrives at the train station. The old man with long white hair, a curly moustache and arms full of tattoos, who is dressed like a biker and rides an electric wheelchair. An endless variety of characters, all different from each other. The diversity and richness of cultures that England has is a big part of why I love to be here.

I escape for a moment from the steady stream of people who come and go, thinking back over my life and the time I have spent – all my experiences in the many years that I have been here. England gave me the opportunity to create the life I wanted, both professionally and personally. I have taken on various roles doing what I enjoy. I have made good friends. I have travelled to many different countries around the world and enjoyed countless wonderful experiences and adventures. I have found love and had my share of broken relationships. I've learned that living alone can be a great delight and bring peace of mind, but I've also learned not to close the door to the heart – you never know who might come to visit.

For now, I live in the present moment and enjoy what I have – my health, my family, my friends and, of course, my work that I love so much. I want to continue doing what I love – supporting people with learning disabilities and making a meaningful difference. Bringing comfort and perhaps, once in a while, bright eyes and a lovely smile.

About me

I was born in Barcelona many years ago. When I was three years old, my parents moved to live in the region of Murcia. There I spent all my childhood and part of my youth. When I was in my early twenties, I told my family that I was going to England for just six months to take a course to improve my English. Twenty years later, my family still wonders how long it will take me to complete that English course. I answer them, "Que será, será" – whatever will be, will be …

Printed in Great Britain
by Amazon

73355716R00069